Anna Ziegler Plays Two

T0382696

For my children, Elliot and Nathaniel

Anna Ziegler Plays Two

The Wanderers
Actually
Another Way Home
The Great Moment

ANNA ZIEGLER

methuen | drama
LONDON • NEW YORK • OXFORD • NEW DELHI • SYDNEY

METHUEN DRAMA
Bloomsbury Publishing Plc
50 Bedford Square, London, WC1B 3DP, UK
1385 Broadway, New York, NY 10018, USA
29 Earlsfort Terrace, Dublin 2, Ireland

BLOOMSBURY, METHUEN DRAMA and the Methuen Drama logo are
trademarks of Bloomsbury Publishing Plc

First published in this collection in Great Britain 2023
Introduction © Anna Ziegler, 2023
The Wanderers © Anna Ziegler, 2023
Actually © Anna Ziegler, 2017
Another Way Home © Anna Ziegler, 2023
The Great Moment © Anna Ziegler, 2023

Cover design by James Illman

A catalogue record for this book is available from the British Library.

A catalog record for this book is available from the Library of Congress.

ISBN: PB: 978-1-3503-4968-1
ePDF: 978-1-3503-4970-4
eBook: 978-1-3503-4969-8

Series: Methuen Drama Play Collections

Typeset by Newgen KnowledgeWorks Pvt. Ltd., Chennai, India
Printed and bound in Great Britain

To find out more about our authors and books visit www.bloomsbury.com
and sign up for our newsletters.

Contents

Introduction, by Anna Ziegler

These are plays about family. *The Great Moment* and *Another Way Home* are explicitly about families, about the rifts and miscommunications that complicate these fragile ecosystems. *The Wanderers* takes on the notion of arranged marriage and questions whether the love that grows out of an arrangement is qualitatively different from other kinds of love. It also has to do with the families we come from, and the baggage we carry when we're away from them, as does *Actually*—the baggage we bring with us into every new interaction, friendship, love affair.

All of these plays, to one degree or another, grapple with how difficult it is to escape our families—but also with whether or not we should want to. It's an idea that feels personally relevant right now. I'm writing this essay on June 27, 2022, as my grandfather, on whom *The Great Moment* is based (much of Max's, the old man's, dialogue is his, verbatim), is dying in a nursing home 200 miles away from me. He is 104 years old. In 2016, when I started writing *The Great Moment*, we also thought he was dying. It's what spurred me to write the play. I wanted to hold onto our family as it was, for just a moment, before things inevitably changed.

My grandfather is a man who is grappling with whether or not to leave. For context, he is a man who holds onto things, even things that are slippery and difficult to hold. He held fiercely to my grandmother through her years of dementia, even when she didn't know him anymore. He holds onto classic poetry and the lyrics of show tunes, and until a year or so ago could still sing to us, as badly as he always did. The last thing he said to my eight-year-old son on our final visit to his nursing home was the line of poetry that was, strangely, their insider catchphrase—"the smith, a mighty man is he"—from Longfellow's *The Village Blacksmith* ("Under a spreading chestnut-tree / the village smithy stands; / the smith, a mighty man is he, / with large and sinewy hands; / and the muscles of his brawny arms / are strong as iron bands…")

My grandfather has held firmly and admirably onto his sense of humor and sense of kindness. He has been unfailingly polite, even to the end, thanking aides for their help, apologizing for dozing off while you talk to him. But, as the sentiment in one of his favorite poems goes: "the art of losing isn't hard to master," he has also lost so much. He has not held onto his hearing or his ability to walk (he broke his hip mid-Covid-19), and his eyesight is too weak to allow him to read. He can't follow his beloved basketball teams or the stock market, the scroll at the bottom of the television screen, the tickertape that hummed along under all of his days.

My mother says he has a strong will to live, which in this case might be synonymous with being afraid of dying.

* * *

These are also plays that have to do with acceptance—with trying to accept and enjoy the life we're given, trying to accept the darker parts of ourselves, and, perhaps more than anything else, trying to accept the passage of time and its consequences. But because freezing time is as impossible as making the most of it, these characters (and their author) are stuck in a limbo of wanting to capture something while also wanting desperately to understand how to let go.

My grandfather, Robert Lewis, was a star basketball player in the 1930s. People recognized him on the streets of New York City. He was also very handsome. My grandmother was beautiful too—an aspiring actress. They seemed to have it all. But of course their story led them into choppier waters. There was the war, and then the injury that meant the end of my grandfather's basketball career, and then difficulty holding down jobs (my grandfather was also sometimes incapable of holding in his temper or sense of righteousness). There were three children and a true and lasting love but also depression, bitterness, too many tchotchkes, and a few years in Colorado everyone would prefer to forget. There is no single snapshot that could capture it all. And yet maybe one does. It's black and white. I'm almost certain my grandfather took it. My mother and her sisters— teenagers—stand in cowboy hats by the side of the road. They stare into the distance, not at the camera. This is a pit stop on the road to Yosemite National Park. The girls, it seems, are looking into the future. And the future, in turn, stares back at them, in the form of the photographer's grandchild, many years later, wondering about those hats, that trip, their lives.

* * *

My grandfather, who loved words and poetry, was tickled by the fact that I wrote plays. That some of them got produced. He used to brag about me in his Florida condominium. There's a story, perhaps apocryphal, in which it turned out the playwright Lauren Gunderson's grandmother (great-aunt?) also lived in his building. Somehow they discovered they'd both sired playwrights. At some point my grandfather described his favorite play of mine to Lauren Gunderson's progenitor, who'd never heard of it.

His favorite play of mine was not the one I wrote in more or less direct homage to him. It's a play called *The Last Match*, and almost every time I would see him, in addition to saying, "You look good. I think you look good, Anna" (even when it was patently untrue), at some point he'd say, "You know, I really do like that play. *The Last Match*. I think you were onto something there." He was a tennis player (he played into his nineties), and fan, and I think he liked that the play was about sports but also about failure, a subject with which he was intimate. I don't actually know what he made of *The Great Moment*. He was too frail to go see it when it premiered in Seattle in the Fall of 2019. He read it, supposedly. Maybe it hit too close to home, being, as it was (and is), a play about an old man struggling to let go. Or maybe this is the nature of family—that we like what we like and are who we are and try to hold onto each other anyway. Maybe a photograph of three young women on the side of a road in the 1960s *can* capture a feeling and a moment that its photographer, my grandfather (like Lillian in *Another Way Home*) knows will be insufficient but takes anyway, because what lies just outside the frame is dark, and scary, and hard to make out, and also why not hold onto things, while you can.

The Wanderers

The Wanderers was originally commissioned, developed, and produced by The Old Globe.
(Barry Edelstein, Artistic Director; Michael G. Murphy, Managing Director)

Director: Barry Edelstein

Cast

Abe	**Daniel Eric Gold**
Sophie	**Michelle Beck**
Julia	**Janie Brookshire**
Schmuli	**Dave Klasko**
Esther	**Ali Rose Dachis**

Stage Manager	Anjee Nero
Scenic	Marion Williams
Costume	David Israel Reynoso
Lighting	Amanda Zieve
Sound	Jane Shaw
Projections	Jeanette Oi-Suk Yew

Opening night was April 13, 2018 at the Old Globe Theatre (San Diego) in the Sheryl and Harvey White Theatre

Characters

Esther—*mid-twenties to early thirties; she feels young, impressionable, eager and yet no-nonsense too; she's Jewish (Hasidic)*
Schmuli—*thirties—formal, not totally comfortable in his skin, also Hasidic; should have the capacity for deep, surprising emotion; he is a profoundly gentle person*
Abe—*mid-thirties to early forties—an intellectual who knows he's an intellectual, enjoys seducing with language, a bit pretentious but charming and not without humor and self-awareness/self-deprecation; he is Caucasian, Jewish*
Sophie—*mid-thirties to early forties—***Abe**'s *wife, dry and intelligent and world-weary; she is half Caucasian/Jewish and half Black*
Julia—*mid-thirties to early forties—a movie star with an abundance of outward charm and confidence and an easy laugh; she is poised and polished, but not without vulnerability*

Time: 1973–1982 and 2015–2017

L'chi Lach to a land that I will show you
Leich L'cha to a place you do not know
                              —Debbie Friedman

Tell me, what else should I have done?
Doesn't everything die at last, and too soon?
Tell me, what is it you plan to do with your one wild and
precious life?
                              —Mary Oliver

There is always a suspicion ... that one is living a lie or a mistake;
that something crucially important has been overlooked, missed,
neglected, left untried and unexplored; that a vital obligation to
one's own authentic self has not been met, or that some chances
of unknown happiness completely different from any happiness
experienced before have not been taken up in time and are bound
to be lost forever.
                              —Esther Perel

The poet appears to have found his subject—the labyrinth of self-
deceit into which we are led by, among other things, language
itself, by the difficult reformulation of one's own story.
          —Margalit Fox "J.D. McClatchy, Poet of the
          Body, in Sickness and Health, Dies at 72," The
                              New York Times

Sophie *stands in a spotlight, perhaps behind a lectern, at a reading.*

Sophie   I was seventeen when I realized I was going to marry Abe. We were driving home from school. I was driving because Abe, even then, was too neurotic. What if he crashed the car and was responsible for something terrible? So I drove. And on this particular day he was reading aloud. This wasn't unusual. Abe loved to read to me. Mostly his own writing, but also passages from his favorite novels; once, at a Foot Locker, he recited the last lines of Philip Roth's *Sabbath's Theater* over and over again, laughing and then ... crying. *And he couldn't do it. He could not fucking die. How could he leave? Everything he hated was here.* And the guy who worked there was looking at me, like "are you sure you're okay?" But I was. And I bought these bright pink high-tops to make my mother worry she would never really know me and to make Abe think I was bold. The day I realized I was going to marry him, we were in the car and he was reading a poem of mine aloud. A poem he'd grabbed out of my backpack, against my will. But the way he read it, with so much reverence for each word, made it sound ... beautiful. And important. And I felt completely ... seen.

Beat.

I was almost forty when I realized I would leave him.

CHAPTER ONE (or, Marriage)

Enter **Esther** *and* **Schmuli**, *dancing, but not together; they stay separate from each other. We are at their wedding. There is something frantic and beautiful about the dance.*

Then it is just after the wedding. Late at night. **Esther** *and* **Schmuli** *are alone together for the very first time.*

Esther   So how did you enjoy our wedding?

Schmuli (*not sure how to answer*)   I thought it was very ... pleasant.

Esther   Yes. It was.

Schmuli   Did you enjoy the dancing, I wonder?

Esther   I wish! All I could think about was keeping this sheitel on; I was praying so hard that it wouldn't fall off.

Schmuli   But it didn't?

Esther (*wryly, with a smile*)   What a merciful God we have, right?

Beat. They both look at the ground.

Esther   I'm sorry. Usually I have a lot to say. Usually people tell me "Enough already, Esther."

Schmuli   You did talk a lot. At our meeting.

Esther   I was so nervous! My Tante Golde said "you're twenty-three, practically dead. If this one isn't a match, you're done for." (*Smiling.*) I guess I can tell you that, now that you're stuck with me.

Schmuli   I'm very pleased to be stuck with you.

Esther   You're sweet. I could tell you were sweet. What could you tell about me?

He doesn't say anything, looks down.

You must've thought *something*.

Schmuli   I thought you had very nice shoes.

Esther   Nice shoes.

Schmuli   Yes.

Esther (*a genuine question, gentle*)   What, did you never look at me?

Schmuli (*reassuring, kind*)   And yet I saw enough.

Esther   You might be crazy, Schmuli Simcha. To marry without even looking.

Schmuli   Not crazy. Only shy.

Esther   And what happens now.

Schmuli   Oh, I um … I mean, we don't have to, um.

Esther   No—I didn't mean *now* now. I know what happens *now* now.

Schmuli   You do?

Esther   I meant in life. Like is this moment the beginning of the rest of our lives?

Schmuli   Isn't that true, every day?

Esther (*hopeful*)   Does it feel that way to you?

Schmuli   Maybe we should just focus on what happens now. One never really knows what anything means. At least not till so much later.

Esther   I see.

Schmuli   It's not just that I only want to … um.

Esther   Have you ever done it before?

Schmuli   Of course I have not done it; what kind of a question is this?

Esther   I have read books about it. I've read books I probably shouldn't have read.

Schmuli   I have a feeling it's different in life than in books.

Esther   How so?

Schmuli   I don't know. When I listen to music I don't have the experience of listening to music that I've read about. And … I've listened to music I probably shouldn't have listened to.

Esther   How do you experience listening to music?

Schmuli   It depends on the music, of course, but.

Esther   But?

Schmuli   It's the closest I've ever come to God.

Esther   Closer than during Neilah, when the gates are closing?

Schmuli   Yes.

Esther   Well, they say … relations between a man and a woman are also supposed to bring one closer to God.

Schmuli   They do say that.

Esther   I'm not eighteen years old, you know. I'm not scared.

Schmuli (*even more terrified*)   So you would like to simply … commence, then?

Esther   Is that how you're going to ask me?

Schmuli   I don't know … How *should* I ask you?

Esther   … Why don't you say my name.

Schmuli   Esther.

Esther   Yes … Say my name and then say … (*She thinks.*) Say: "come to me."

Schmuli (*awkward*)   Esther. Come to me.

Esther   No, it doesn't sound right. Can you think of anything?

Schmuli   How about "are you ready to commence?"

Esther   You did that one already.

Schmuli   Did I?

Esther   Yes.

Now we meet **Abe**, *who's on a total high. He and* **Sophie** *are at home, in Brooklyn.*

Sophie   She didn't really write to you.

Abe   Look: yes-its-me-the-real-julia-cheever at gmail.com.

Sophie   That isn't really her. That can't be her actual email address.

Abe   Sure it is. She's being ironic. And I know you'll laugh at me, but I'm not entirely surprised that she wrote. I mean, she sat right up front at the reading. She wanted me to see her. She was engaging me, somehow.

Sophie   Yes I will laugh at you.

Abe   Well, if you didn't laugh mercilessly at me everyday I'd think something was terribly wrong.

Sophie   Let me see the email.

Abe   It's private.

She shoots him a look—she's not messing around. He hands **Sophie** *his laptop.*

Then: **Julia** *in spotlight.*

Julia   Dear Abe—can I call you Abe? I hope it's not wrong of me to write. Or presumptuous.

But I heard you read last week and I haven't been able to stop thinking about it. James, my husband, is one of your biggest fans, and I admit—he dragged me along with him. I don't usually go to book readings. As you can imagine I can't go anywhere in public without a hassle—

Sophie   Seriously? She can't go anywhere "without a hassle"? Come on.

Abe   Well, it's probably true.

Sophie   Also it *is* kind of presumptuous, don't you think? Just to write you, out of the blue.

Abe   Except she's not wrong. I was thrilled to hear from her.

Sophie   You really think she's that pretty?

Abe   Luminous.

Sophie   Please don't hold back on my account.

Julia   And also, and really more to the point, aren't most book readings mind-numbingly boring? But not yours. And I would say I loved what you read—which I did—but even more I loved what you *said*. About the never-ending conflict between the head and the heart, between the private and the public self, between what we think we want and what we actually have. I found you very … appealing. Is that wrong of me to express? Well, screw it—that's how I felt. And I know you've been accused of writing unlikeable characters but I'll say this—if your characters are anything like you, then I think your critics are wrong.

Then a change in tone—lighter.

Anyway, I guess I'll read your books now. Or at least add one to the stack on my bedside table, so I'll always be *about* to begin. Ha ha. Yours sincerely, Julia

Sophie   And you really think that's her.

Abe   You don't?

Beat.

Or you just don't believe Julia Cheever could find me appealing?

Sophie   Yeah, both. I don't think it's her and I don't think she would find you appealing.

Abe   Really, the danger now, for you, is that someone on the list is actually within reach.

Sophie   I'll remember to be worried, thank you.

Abe (*joking*)   You know what? I'm feeling generous. I think I'll let you have Dan Rather. He took such a shine to you at that NEA luncheon.

Sophie   Oh I'd take Brokaw over Rather.

Abe   Sure, that gravelly voice, that wholesome Midwestern trustworthiness. Like so many men of a certain era. Whereas Julia Cheever could only be Julia Cheever. She doesn't seem like anyone else.

Sophie   You don't know her. You know that, right?

Abe   Let's go dancing.

Sophie   We don't go dancing. That is not something that we do.

Abe   But we could. Wouldn't it be nice to do something novel? Maybe we could even drink and do drugs.

Sophie (*scoffing*)   "Do drugs."

Then, interested.

Which drugs?

Abe   I don't know. Nicotine. What do you say?

Sophie (*snapping her fingers*)   Oh shoot. I just remembered those small children sleeping in the other room. We can't leave them in the house alone. It's frowned upon by the law and also they might kill each other.

Abe   Right. Fine. Then do you want to have sex?

Sophie (*without missing a beat*)   No.

Abe (*also without missing a beat*)   Okay.

Sophie   I'm gonna go to bed.

Abe   Already?

Sophie   … I have kind of a big day tomorrow.

He can't remember what she's referring to.

You have no clue what I'm talking about.

Abe   No. I do.

Sophie   Then what. What am I doing tomorrow?

He kisses her tenderly on the cheek.

Abe   Have I told you how much I love you? That I couldn't survive without you?

Sophie   I have a meeting with that editor.

Abe   Yes! Of course. The meeting with the editor. The young one, right?

Sophie   Well, it's a new imprint.

Abe   … So you're going to write another book. That's the plan?

Beat.

Sophie (*touchy*)   I don't know, Abe. I don't know if I'll write another book. It's just a meeting.

Abe   Well, you don't have to. If you don't want to.

Sophie   Thanks for that.

She turns to go.

Abe   No, don't go.

Sophie (*suddenly cutting*)   Are *you* gonna write another book?

Beat.

Abe   Why wouldn't I?

Sophie   Exactly.

Sophie *exits;* **Abe** *immediately writes back.*

Abe   Julia Cheever. I didn't really believe it when I saw your name in my inbox, like an answered prayer. My wife assumed it was a hoax. But who would know that I've admired you so all these years? So I won't over-think things, as is my wont. Also, for the record, it's *women* I'm accused of making unlikeable. Apparently I couldn't recognize a real woman if she was staring me in the face.

CHAPTER TWO (Or, Children)

Schmuli and Esther are in her hospital room. She's recently given birth to their first child, who is in a bassinet next to her bed.

Schmuli I am just ... amazed really. *Hodu L'Hashem Kitov Ki Leolam Chasdo.*

Esther (*looking down at the baby, overwhelmed/humbled*) I know ... It's incredible.

Schmuli And you ... I mean, you were so ... I was so impressed.

Esther You weren't even in the room!

Schmuli One moment you were shrieking so loud I thought my eardrums would burst—

Esther Okay, I'm not so sure I need to relive all that—

Schmuli And I was reciting the Psalms over and over again—

Esther You did say those Psalms an awful lot. I could hear you.

Schmuli Psalm 20 is thought to be particularly good for easing the pangs of labor. Nine verses for nine months of being with child. Seventy words for the seventy pains of labor.

Esther Were there only seventy?

Schmuli I must've recited them fifteen times.

Esther You must have.

Schmuli My mouth got tired. My tongue was very dry.

Esther I'm sorry your mouth got tired and your tongue was dry.

Schmuli I didn't want to take any of your ice chips; you seemed in desperate need of them.

Esther Do you want to hold her?

He keeps a certain distance away.

Come on; she won't bite. No teeth.

Schmuli But is it permitted?

Esther She's your daughter, Schmuli. Who cares if it's permitted?

Schmuli   … No she's sleeping. I won't disturb her. God willing there will be much time for me to hold her. Our little little. Our *n'shomela.*

Esther   *Ein ba'al ha-nes makir b'niso.*

Schmuli   It's true. We are very blessed.

Esther   Should you go daven? It's late.

Schmuli   Yes.

But he doesn't move.

Esther   What is it, Schmuli. Nu?

Schmuli   I wonder if you feel the same as you did before. Or if God has moved through you so that now you are filled with his light.

Esther (*laughing a little*)   "Filled with light?" No I feel tired! That's what I feel.

Schmuli (*chastened*)   Okay.

Esther (*then, gentler*)   No. I mean, of course it is a miracle. Here is this baby, and I don't know where she came from. But also, at the same time, the pain, and I'm sorry, but the blood, and I threw up on the doctor's shoes, and there were so many instruments inside me I was like an orchestra. So, no … it wasn't just light and holiness, Schmuli. I'm sorry.

Schmuli   No *I'm* sorry. I know I never say the right things.

Esther (*gently*)   Just go daven. Tell the family and receive their blessings.

Schmuli   Okay, I will. But Esther.

Esther   What?

Schmuli   Can I just say … The thing I was going to say … the thing I wanted to say …

Esther   Go on.

Schmuli   One moment you were shrieking and the next moment … there she was, and the way she cried out was like a song, like a question, and the answer was: yes, I will care for you the rest of my life.

The lights shift. **Julia** *and* **Abe** *are emailing.*

Julia   Holy shit, Abe, you wrote back! It made my day. I'm sitting in my trailer, on the set of "Everyman"—the new Philip Roth adaptation—just glowing. Certainly not because of the content of the movie, which is as bleak as you would expect, but because there was some part of me that presumed you wouldn't have any interest in me. I don't have your way with words, after all.

Abe   Come on. You have all the *other* things. All I've got are words. And even those fail me much of the time. A relevant example: in the hours since receiving your email I composed fourteen different responses. Any that tried to play it cool failed miserably. I can't pretend I'm not fascinated by everything about you. And I don't mean the being famous part, though of course I'm interested in that too, but mostly it's the daily stuff. How a presumably regular person lives this irregular life. How you have a marriage and two children—and please forgive me for knowing more about you than I should but I think it would be an insult to feign ignorance when all any of us should be doing with our time is following your every move. I am kidding, of course. Mostly. Though not about wanting to know who you are. I suppose the question is: how do you get through the day, Julia Cheever?

Sophie   Hey, so.

Abe *looks up, shifts his focus. There's* **Sophie**.

Abe   Oh I didn't see you there. Did you put the kids to bed?

Sophie   Who else would have?

Abe   Is that like a dig?

Sophie   So I need to work tomorrow.

Abe   Okay.

Sophie   No, I mean, you'll need to wake up with the kids, make breakfast, take them to school, pick them up.

Abe   You need to work all day?

Sophie   That's right. All day.

Abe   Let's just get a sitter then.

Sophie   I don't want to spend the next three hours trying to find a sitter. You can, if you want to. *Or* you can just not do your work for a bit tomorrow, and let me do mine.

Abe   What's going on, Sophie.

Beat.

Sophie (*embarrassed to bring this up*)   I'm not sure if ... I mean, can I even call myself a writer anymore?

Abe   Of course you can.

Sophie   Even if I *never* do it? I don't know. Everything is just so simple for you—

Abe   Nothing is simple for me.

Sophie   You're right, getting a Pulitzer and two National Book Awards before turning thirty is pretty rough.

Abe   I can't re-read *A Theory of Milk* without wanting to kill myself. Its pretentiousness is staggering. And *Orphan of Vilnius* is a work of sheer genius (*he smiles*) but I'm still gonna die one day.

Sophie   Abe.

Abe   And before that be subjected to routine colonoscopies.

Sophie   I'm grinding my teeth again. This morning I woke up and it felt like there'd been a war in my mouth.

Abe   Like when Robby was born.

Sophie   And when my book came out ... I mean, I worked so hard on it and for what?

Abe   It's an objectively beautiful book.

Sophie   It is. That's the tragedy of it all.

Abe   You did for Vietnamese villagers what Faulkner did for the American South.

Sophie   I researched the shit out of that novel.

Abe   It showed.

Sophie   What does that mean?

Abe (*not letting her goad him into a fight*)   Can I say something and not have you bite my head off? Something you already know.

Sophie   What.

Abe   It won't make you happy. The writing. Not ever.

Sophie   No, that's you, honey.

Abe   You will feel like someone else's book is better. You will feel misunderstood and underappreciated. You will feel certain your best work is behind you but even that wasn't good enough. You will feel like a failure no matter what so don't try to write what you think they want to read. You, Sophie, are so interesting. I mean—all the *inherited trauma*; how many people can claim a legacy of the Holocaust *and* slavery.

Sophie   But I don't want to write about myself. I write to get away from myself. Also, slavery and the Holocaust don't define me. I grew up in Albany. The only place I ever wanted to escape was that weird music camp my Mom made me go to.

Abe   Well you don't have to write about any of it explicitly.

Sophie   But I'm not even sure I wanna write! That's what I'm trying to say. I don't know what I want. Sometimes I even wonder if I might want another baby—

Abe (*not unkindly*)   I thought we'd settled this.

Sophie   I don't wanna *not* do something and then regret it later on.

Abe   You really wanna put ourselves through all of that again just because it might be theoretically nice to have more children around some abstract, future Thanksgiving Day table?

Sophie   But maybe it *would* be nice.

Abe   Come on, Soph. You think anyone with more than two kids is certifiable.

Sophie   I do. I really do … I'm just looking for something, I think.

Abe   I know. We all are.

Sophie   My mother says I enable you. That I'm scared to do my own work so I tell myself yours is more important. And she's right. So why do you let me do it? Because you're protecting me from getting hurt again or because it makes your life so easy?

Breath.

Abe   Both, probably. If I'm honest, probably both.

Back to emailing; days later.

Julia   How do I get through the day? Gosh, Abe, I don't know. Same as you I'd imagine. There's a little added glamor, which gets old quickly, and many additional difficulties that never do, but mostly it's the mundane stuff. My son Bishop is almost three; the baby, Essex, is six months old, and I feel very lucky to be their mom. I know that's cheesy as hell. But it's true. And James and I have been married ten years now. So a lot of that is about finding ways to re-see each other, if that makes sense.

Abe   Wow. I wish Sophie and I could "re-see" each other. Mostly our relationship is fueled by an unspoken competition around who reads the most features in the New Yorker in a given week and who the kids love more. Right now it's me, and she hates it. But it's easier to be a father. Mothers are supposed to be everything to everyone. I get points if I just, like, show up to dinner.

Julia   You're right—it is harder to be a mother. Cut your wife some slack. Tell your children to be nicer to her. Every time Bishop sees a suitcase he sobs. He doesn't make it easy for me to go away. Not that it should be easy to leave him.

Abe   Sure, the guilt is terrible. I feel guilty when I'm in the bathroom too long, let alone on a book tour. I can't even get myself on a plane, not since the kids were born. All I can think of is that second when you realize the thing is going down and you'll never see them again. That your final moments would just be full of this terrible self-recrimination about leaving them without a father.

Julia   But flying is safer than driving. Everyone knows that.

Abe   Oh, logic has absolutely nothing to do with the decisions I make. It drives my wife crazy.

Julia   Is she supportive? Of your writing?

Abe   Totally. And also not at all. It's tricky. She's a writer too; she published a novel a decade ago and it got dismal reviews and then disappeared, which was incredibly disheartening for her especially in light of my success … See, there is a small, or perhaps not so small, way in which my wife hates me, but also can't, and it tortures her.

Julia   Does she know we're writing to each other?

Abe   Oh.
Yes.
More or less.
Maybe not the *entire* extent of it.
But she teases me. She says I need this to stave off a mid-life crisis.

Julia   My husband thinks I'm trying to ingratiate myself to you so I can be in your next film adaptation.

Abe   Well, it's working.

Julia   Good.

Abe   You know … If a day passes and I haven't heard from you I get … jumpy. It's like I can't focus.

Beat.

Julia   Abe, I'm not sure what to …

Abe   No.
Ignore me.
I'm an idiot.
I'm just so enjoying becoming your friend.
I can't tell you what your movies have done for me.
All of them, but especially the ones when I was a teenager. Those were formative.
You were this girl my age who was so smart but also beautiful but also attainable.
You made things seem … possible. Even though my home life was so …

Julia   So … what?

Abe   Sophie would say a train wreck. I'd say it was complicated.

Julia   So you and Sophie knew each other when you were kids?

The lights shift. **Abe** *rehearses a speech.*

Abe (*to the audience*)   I don't think there was ever a time when I didn't know Sophie.

We grew up together. Our *mothers* grew up together, Hasidic Jews in Williamsburg, Brooklyn. Mine escaped not long after she had me. Sophie's got out much earlier.

So Soph and I are the products of very particular women … Recklessly brave women.

After all, it's not easy to leave a sect like the Satmars. They'll cut you off; one by one they'll snip the delicate threads that constitute your identity. When I was a baby, my mother had nothing. So yeah, Soph and I met before memory. Before anything is recorded and turned into a story. We were best friends. We went to middle school prom together, where I tried the whole time to dance with Sarah Winters, a snub for which I have yet to be forgiven, and we'd have gone to senior prom too if Soph hadn't gotten Lyme disease and been laid up for three weeks watching so much *90210* she cycled completely through loving Dylan and then Brandon and then back to Dylan again. I brought her chicken soup that was inedible because I made it myself. We got engaged on my twenty-seventh birthday.

Sophie (*entering*)   Huh.

Abe   What do you mean "huh"?

Sophie   For one thing—that was terrible, when I had Lyme disease. So don't glorify it.

Abe   Was I glorifying it?

Sophie   I don't know, Abe ...

Abe   That's never the start of something that ends well. It's never: "I don't know, Abe. I just think you're awesome."

Sophie   It's always just ... weird. To hear our story as this, like, sound byte. It feels fundamentally ... dishonest.

Abe   Because it is.

Sophie   But like to casually mention our mothers in that way?

Abe   These are patrons at the 92nd Street Y, not paid psychoanalysts.

Sophie   I wish you *would* see a shrink. You know that.

Abe   I already lead the most examined life of anyone I know. I don't think I could take much more.

Sophie   All the dreams. And the fights you had with your mom. And the dreams about the fights you had with your mom. Religion was loaded for her so it's loaded for you. / I get it.

Abe (*that word is such an understatement*)   Loaded?

Sophie   But right now there's nothing actually holding you to it. So just believe or don't believe. It doesn't have to be such a big deal.

Abe   Of course you think that. You're not Jewish.

Sophie (*they've had this discussion many times before*)   I'm half Jewish, Abe.

Abe   Okay but you don't think of yourself as Jewish. You weren't brought up that way.

Sophie   Unitarian is kind of like Jewish.

Abe   Our children wouldn't know from Jewish if it weren't for me.

Sophie   I will never understand why you want to raise our kids in a religion you hate.

Abe   Because that's what Jews do!

Sophie   I mean, do you really need a whole prepared answer about how we met?

Abe   Oh, they always ask how your life affects your art on these kinds of panels. And you, my liebling, are my whole life.

Sophie (*flirty*)   … Am I?

Abe   Can I tell you something?

Sophie   What.

Abe   I want us to re-see each other.

Sophie   Re-see each other.

Abe   I've been thinking about you.

Sophie   What kind of thinking?

Abe   Fantasizing.

Sophie   Abe.

Abe   No, I have been. I wanna … do things to you we've never done before.

Sophie   Like what?

Abe   Unspeakable things. Right now.

Sophie   Right now?

Abe   Yeah.

CHAPTER THREE (or, Boredom)

Schmuli *enters, home from work.* **Esther** *is listening to the radio and shuts it off as soon as he enters, but not soon enough.*

Esther (*covering, a little eager*)   So the girls are asleep, finally. You should have heard Leah tonight—Why why why. Why do I have to go to bed. But *why* do I need sleep to grow big. Why do I need to grow at all, why can't I just stay a child? She's a little nudga with all her questions ...

Schmuli   What were you listening to?

Esther   What?

Schmuli (*with affection*)   Nu, will you really deny it?

Esther   I wasn't listening to—

Schmuli (*interrupting*)   I hope it wasn't FM. FM is worse.

Esther (*smiling—she's caught him*)   How would *you* know that.

Schmuli   Do you listen to the radio often?

Esther   No. . .

(*Mischevously.*) Yes.

Schmuli   How often.

Esther   I get bored.

Schmuli   How often do you get bored.

Esther   I'd like to get a computer.

Schmuli   What? What kind of mishegoss is this? No one we know has a computer.

Esther   Who says we can't be the first?

Schmuli   Also we can't afford a computer.

Esther   How about I get a job and then we get a computer.

Schmuli   Okay you have gone off the deep end. *Gornisht helfn.*

Esther   Many women have jobs. Rachy Heschel works the reception desk at her husband's insurance agency.

Schmuli   It is run out of their tiny home. I think the desk might be the only place for her to sit all day.

Esther   I'm serious.

Schmuli   And will it end there, Esther?

Esther   What.

Schmuli   If you get a job. If we get a computer, will it end there?

Esther   I don't know. I'm not a prophet. Also I don't *want* to know what life has in store. It's too boring that way. Also … I don't like listening to you chew your food, and at night your breathing keeps me awake. Sometimes I wish the breathing would just stop, which is not the same as wishing you dead, I swear. Also, how was your day? Has Rev Moshul's rash begun to fade? Did you get to have lunch outside in the park? I always think of you eating lunch in the park and I am sick with envy.

Schmuli   It is not so wonderful, eating in the park. The pigeons are aggressive and I shvitz like crazy.

Esther   You should get a lighter rekel.

Schmuli   Who can afford it?

Esther   With the money from my *job*, I will get it for you.

Schmuli   And who will take care of Leah and Miriam? No. Wait until our children are grown. Then maybe you get a job.

Esther   And spend the next fifteen years at the mercy of Faigy Gurkow who comes down every hour to ask if I smell gas? At which point we check her burners and as always they are off—no gas.

Schmuli   It will be as Ha-Shem wants it. This is how our parents, our grandparents, our great-grandparents all went.

Esther   Whose voice is coming out of your mouth. Yours? Or your father's? Meyn schver, who thinks my eyes should never meet his. Who told my tateh his contribution was not raised right—"contribution," Schmuli.

Schmuli   Well, *I* don't think of you that way.

Esther   You are under his thumb. You would never say a word against him.

Schmuli   Why should I upset him?

Esther   In the years when you were in Israel, after yeshiva, did you not see other ways of life?

He doesn't say anything.

You were sent there, were you not, because you were questioning things. So maybe our daughter takes after her father.

Schmuli   Or her mother, more like.

One day, B'esras Ha-Shem, we will have a son and perhaps he will take after me.

The lights shift. **Abe** *and* **Julia** *are instant messaging.*

Julia   Oh good, you're there.

I've been looking for you.

Abe   Have you. Wow. How are you?

Julia   The nanny is home sick and both kids are sick and I can't get cast by Terrence Malick to save my life and this morning I lost it at my assistant and she started to *cry*. So that's how I am.

Abe (*with total seriousness*)   Holy shit you are, like, a terrible person.

Julia (*smiling*)   Don't say that!

Abe   No, I'm on your side. And you know what? I'll even take it upon myself to cheer you up. I am after all known for being very cheery.

Julia   Are you?

Abe   Not at all. But I like a challenge.

Julia   Tell me something cheerful then.

Abe   Okay … how about when something you assume will go terribly wrong is not a total unmitigated disaster. For me that would be … my books. Also my children. Also dental work.

Julia   Not bad.

Abe   A close second might be when a barber or Uber driver or dermatologist doesn't make me talk to them.

Julia (*with joking disbelief*)   Really? There are times when *you* don't wanna talk?

Abe   Oh my god, I never wanna talk. I can literally think of nothing better than seeing "can't make lunch today" pop up on your phone, which means you get to just stay home, and not talk.

Julia   But your children might be there and you might have to talk to them.

Abe   Robby I could do without—ha ha—but Esther is fun. She has ideas all of a sudden. She has a worldview. I don't know where it came from.

Julia   Esther's a pretty name.

Abe   Snow days! Those are cheery. I'm not sure I've ever been happier than those mornings in childhood when you'd wake up and suddenly have the whole day ahead of you ...

Julia   Dark chocolate with sea salt. Margaritas with salt around the rim. Corn on the cob coated in salt. If you catch my theme ...

Abe   Mozart's Overture to the *Marriage of Figaro*. Anything by Art Garfunkel—I'm a total Garfunkel guy—or Jay-Z. I love Jay-Z.

Julia   How about when a Cate Blanchett movie bombs.

Abe   Has that ever happened?

Julia   But think of how it would feel if it did.

Abe   The last sentence of a book you love. Gossiping about a book you hate.

Julia   "The conductor raised his baton, and in that moment Isaac saw his own existence through new eyes, as though a tourist of the strange and beautiful topography that was his life. He would find some way to endure this happiness. The conductor lowered his baton ... and Isaac played."

Abe   Oh my god.

Julia   I couldn't put it down.

Abe   I don't know what to, um ... I'm overwhelmed.

Julia   I loved it. Every word. *I* was overwhelmed ...

(*Really giving him this gift.*)

I think you're a genius, Abe.

Abe   You. You are by far the cheeriest thing I can think of.

Beat.

Julia   What would your wife say if she knew you flirted with me so shamelessly.

Abe   That seems like a dangerous game to play. The what-would-my-wife-think-of-all-of-this game.

Julia   But you wanna play it.

Abe   Absolutely.

Julia   Well.

Abe   Of course I've given this some thought. And what I imagine she would think amounts to a kind of condescending pity that would extend into a grudging sort of acceptance or even permission. Like, if this is how Abe wants to get his jollies, he should just have at it.

Julia   She's a tough one, your wife.

Abe   That's putting it mildly.

Julia   She's very pretty, if that's not a weird thing to say.

Abe   I suppose it's only weird coming from one of the most beautiful women in the world, which is objectively true according to *People* magazine and every man I've ever met. I feel like I'm corresponding with Helen of Troy. *"Why, what could she have done, being what she is? Was there another Troy for her to burn?"*

Julia   What is that? *The Iliad*?

Abe   Yeats.

Julia   You're trying to impress me.

Abe   Of course. And would you believe me if I said it was the only poem I know? That I use it whenever I need to sound smart?

Julia   No.

Abe   You're right. I'm insufferable. I know lots of poems.

Julia   Show off.

Abe   Only when I feel out of my depth. I mean, I don't know why you're engaging in this ... correspondence, or whatever we should call it.

It's obvious why I am, even if it makes me into a bit of a cliché. But you. Talk about mixing with the hoi polloi. Everyday I think: is she done with me now?

Julia   … Not yet.

The lights shift.

CHAPTER FOUR (or, Rivka)

Esther   My best friend Rivka was quiet and full of fantasies—just as
I was. So many afternoons of our childhood turned into evening while
we sat together and read. And yes, we got books from the library even
though it was forbidden. This is how I came to know Ramona Quimby
and Winnie the Pooh, and later Josephine March, Elizabeth Bennet.
Sometimes Rivka would sigh while reading and I'd say, "nu, what is it?"
But one comes to see that it is very hard to explain a passage in a book
that someone else has never read.

Rivka was so invisible in her home she could use it to her advantage;
sometimes she would even go into Manhattan, to museums. And so it
was that leaning over to tie her shoe in the Temple of Dendur, she met
Harold. Harold was not Jewish. Harold was *African-American*. Harold
taught environmental science at the University of Albany. Needless
to say he did not fit in with the community. I heard the most shameful
things said about it. Awful. So Rivka left. Off the derech. People said
she'd lost it—*gornisht helfn*. But if Rivka and Harold don't have the
most beautiful children in the world. And if Rivka is not one of the
happiest women I know. I mean, if she's crazy, then sign me up for the
asylum.

Once I persuaded Schmuli—never very difficult—to let me visit her.
I was twenty-eight and pregnant with our third child. When I arrive, she
won't let me help with anything, even though she has little Sophie, only
one month in the world, and two older kids, who don't lift a finger. And
one night, after the children are finally asleep, she pours herself a very
full glass of wine and says she is no longer spiritual, but if she were
she would create a blessing over *this*—and she takes a small circular
case from a drawer. She says these are pills that stop the body from
conceiving a child. I stare at them. She has had her last baby, she tells
me, laughing. But I don't find it so funny. There will of course always be
a last baby, but I'd prefer not to know that while I am nursing him, while
I am holding him in my arms in the middle of the night. Rivka shrugs.
"Willful ignorance. An abdication of your power. But suit yourself."

And one morning, while Harold cooks *bacon,* and the children read the
newspaper—the children!—my friend asks me what I want. I say "no
bacon for me, thank you" and she smiles—no, she meant in life. Out of
life. Just then the baby kicks, and I know all of a sudden it is a boy, my
first and only boy … my last child, and there he is, sitting at the table

with me, an old man whom I will never know. He looks at me with sad eyes filled with all the things that happen after I am gone. He says to me: "Mameh, did you get the things you wanted?" I don't know how to respond. Who really understands whether or not they are happy?

The lights shift. **Julia** *and* **Abe** *are instant messaging.*

Julia   So I'm sure you know that "Everyman" just came out. And that it bombed. The press just *loathed* it. I always know how badly a movie has gone when I don't hear from anyone. But I thought at least I'd hear from you.

Abe   Okay. First of all, I don't read reviews.

Julia   Yes you do.

Abe   No, I don't. I couldn't care less about them. And for the record, I can't wait to see your movie. I mean, Julia Cheever and Philip Roth? I'm gonna watch it everyday. I'm gonna go to sleep to it and I'm gonna wake up to it. You *think* I'm kidding.

Julia   But, Abe, the movie really *is* bad—

Abe   No it's not. And also that's giving them way too much power.

Julia   Like you've ever been panned.

Abe   Julia, Google "Abe Hausman" and "overrated" and see what you find. People hate me. They hate every idea I've ever put into the world. Every word. They're offended by my very existence.

Julia   Right: everyone's terrible. We all lose. This isn't helping.

Abe   I'm sorry.

Julia (*ignoring him*)   I mean, Roth adaptations are never any good. But I thought this one was reaching for something more interesting. How Everyman leaves wife after wife in search of ... what? In the end he's just left with all this regret about spending his life on these failed families instead of pursuing his art. He decides, at a certain point, to paint a painting and it's the first time we see him *smile*. So doesn't that mean it's a valid choice, sometimes, to be selfish?

Abe   *Of course* you have to be selfish. I mean, truly, what is there in this world to have faith in *besides* the self? Certainly not humanity, which is filled with real cruelty and the performance of cruelty, and death. Certainly not God—how can anyone believe in him? The ultimate in unreliability—

Sophie (*from offstage, interrupting him*)   Abe? ... Abe? Where are you?

Abe (*to* **Julia**)   I have to go, but please don't feel bad. It would kill me to think you're out there feeling bad. You're amazing; you're a force of nature; you bring grown men to their knees. You're not capable of making anything that sucks.

Sophie *enters.*

Sophie   ... What're you doing?

Abe   Working.

Sophie   Yeah. Me too. Wanna take a break?

Abe   Not really.

Sophie   ... You in a groove or something?

Abe   Or something.

He doesn't say anything.

Sophie   What, you want me to go?

He gives her a genuine kiss on the cheek, apologetic.

Abe   Maybe we'll take a break a bit later?

Sophie (*hurt, but trying not to show it*)   Oh. Okay.

She leaves, then turns back.

Sophie   Hey, how's Julia Cheever?

Abe   She's sad her movie was a bust.

Sophie   Oh. Poor her.

Abe   Yeah. It sucks.

Sophie   I bet.

Sophie *leaves.*

Abe   Are you there?

No one responds.

Julia? Did I lose you? Julia?

The lights shift. **Schmuli** *in spotlight.*

Schmuli   One night, after working late, I walked home from the office in new snow. It covered everything and was still pure, the way a night snow is before morning. There is no other way to say it—our little corner of the city felt full of magic, as though Ha-Shem had swept through and touched every forehead. "All is calm all is bright" goes the song; (*with a knowing smile.*) yes, I know it, and it was that sort of night—mid-December. I wanted to stand on my tiptoes and whisper "kadosh kadosh kadosh" into the sky. But all of a sudden I was crying. Why? Because I realized in that moment that I never felt this way in shul. What did *I* find holy? My wife's back as she stood over the pots on the stove, trying not to over-cook anything. *Music.* Especially, I admit, Brahms, Beethoven ... Mozart. The faces of my little daughters, the way, when they slept, you could see all the afternoons of your life.

Sophie   Abe. Abe, wake up.

She is gently shaking him, trying to wake him.

Schmuli   And then the doors to the shul opened and released the men from evening prayers, still aglow with the last words of the Amidah. In their hats and tallesem, and lit by the snow under their feet, these most pious of our men were a sea of black and white, as though things could be that simple. My father was among them.

Sophie   Abe. Wake up. Wake up, honey.

Schmuli   Sometimes, when I was in Israel, I pretended I was someone else. An army man standing guard in front of a bank, a restaurant, a checkpoint. I mean what a *thing*, to hold a gun. If I ever have a boy, I would like for him to be less ... gentle than I am. I would wish for him that his wife respects him. I would like him to be armed with words.

Sophie   Abe.

Abe   What is it? What time is it? I fell asleep.

Sophie   It got late. It's nearly 6 o'clock.

Abe   I'm sorry ... I'm sort of ... in a daze. I think I was having the strangest dream.

Sophie   Abe your father died.

Abe   What?

Sophie   I'm so sorry. Your father died.

She is crying now, a little.

Abe   I don't understand.

Sophie   Your aunt left a message. He was out walking, she said. In the snow. He slipped. Apparently he'd been staring at the sky.

Abe   That's not possible.

Sophie   I know, it's ...

Abe   No.

Sophie   Abe.

Abe   I can't comprehend it.

Sophie   I don't think you have to comprehend it right away.

Abe   ... Maybe I should be alone. Should I be alone?

Sophie   Sure, whatever you ... I'm so sorry, Abe.

She exits. **Abe** *sits with his thoughts. Soon he begins to rock back and forth.*

Abe (*under his breath ... he has trouble remembering the prayer*)   *Yitgadal v'yitkadash sh'mei raba ...*

(*Starting over.*)

Yitgadal v'yitkadash sh'mei raba ... b'alma ...

He puts his head in his hands. After a few moments he opens his eyes.

Abe (*with desperation*)   Are you there? Are you there, Julia? I need you. Julia.

At first nothing—but then she appears.

Julia   Hey there you. What's up.

Abe *lets out one great heaving sob.*

Abe (*quietly, more to himself*)   Behind my eyes all I can see is a black coat on the white snow, like a shadow of a man.

Julia   What's happened, Abe.

Abe   And I didn't even know him. Not really.

Julia   Know who?

Abe   I don't have any parents, I ... (*and then realizing it.*) Oh my god, I don't have any ...

He crumples.

Julia Abe you have me. You have people. You're not alone. Whatever's happened ...

Abe It's horrible, Julia. Life is short, and full of illusion. There is no order to be made from madness. I haven't said it before but I'm saying it now ... I want to see you.

CHAPTER FIVE (or, Fathers and Sons)

Esther *is lying in a hospital bed.*

Schmuli (*excited*) There is just so much to do!

Esther Too much to do.

Schmuli Don't worry, mommellah. I'll work out the details. First the shulem zucher—

Esther Okay that is just for you to drink too much and gossip with the men.

Schmuli And eat peanuts! Don't forget the peanuts.

Esther How could I.

Schmuli The vach nacht the following night. And then the bris of course. Three days later the shlishi lemilah.

Esther There was none of this for the girls.

Schmuli Exactly! This is a true celebration! Oh, if you could have seen my father's face when I told him.

Esther Was he happier than when Leah and Miriam were born?

Schmuli So much happier.

Esther *smiles, thinly.*

Esther I don't know. Maybe we don't do all of it. Maybe we don't follow every single rule for every single celebration.

Schmuli No no we will do *every single* celebration. This is my son! And then the celebrations around his first day in cheder, first haircut, first lesson in Torah. His Bar Mitzvah! Oh what a day that will be. The celebrations, they will never end!

Esther … Well I suppose you should enjoy it while it lasts.

Schmuli What does that mean?

Esther (*offhanded, trying to be casual*) I don't know for certain that we will have more children.

Schmuli Of course we will. Why wouldn't we?

Esther I just don't know, Schmuli. If I want to.

I might like to go to school to become a librarian. I think it would be nice to spend my day surrounded by books.

Schmuli   Goyishe books!

Esther   There are ways to avoid having children, you know.

Schmuli (*pleading with her*)   But it is God's will that we have as many children as we can.

Esther   And yet there's a pill. One wonders: could it exist if God hadn't created it, too?

Schmuli   … Where is this all … No, you're tired. I shouldn't have come to talk to you at this particular moment. It can wait.

Esther   It's just conversation, Schmuli.

Schmuli (*impulsively, out of nowhere*)   My mother says the women talk about you, you know.

Esther   Is that right.

Schmuli   Yes.

Esther   Well, they talk about everyone. That's all the women do is talk.

Schmuli   I'll let you rest now.

Esther   No—wait. I have a name for our son.

Schmuli   Well but we must consult with the rebbe first.

Esther   But I know it! It was my grandfather's. He fled the pogroms when he was a boy and came to America alone, with nothing, and still he made a life.

Schmuli   Come now, let's not be hasty—it must be approved.

Esther *speaks to the baby.*

Esther (*to the baby*)   Hello Abraham. I'm your mother.

Schmuli   Well, now you've said it.

Esther (*quietly*)   And God said to Abraham: "L'ech l'cha. Go for yourself from your land to a land that I will show you."

Schmuli   Let his name be for a blessing.

Esther (*to the baby*)   But God went only partway with Abraham. The rest of the way he had to find on his own.

Schmuli   Esther—

Esther   L'dor vador. From generation to generation we go.

The lights shift.

Abe (*unhinged/fevered*)   So there's a scene in *Anna Karenina* where
Kitty, Levin's wife, is giving birth, and at some point during the hours of
her agonizing labor he realizes that what he's feeling is not unlike what
he felt at his brother's deathbed. That these two experiences constitute
"the loopholes" of life, through which you can glimpse something
higher, something real. And, Julia, it's true. I mean, the sight of my
father's body was like having a debate with someone who makes a point
that suddenly obliterates your entire thesis. I looked at that body and
I thought—well, you can't argue with that. At the funeral I stuck out like
a sore thumb. I was surrounded by relatives I'd never met, who stared at
me shamelessly as though I was to blame, but for what?? I didn't know
my father! Everything he did confused me, or scared me! Everything
he said, everything he wore. Once he even took me to Williamsburg.
I was eleven. And it's not like my dad and I went places together, or saw
each other more than a couple times a year. On the way there he played
classical music and at the end of each seemingly interminable piece,
he'd say:

Schmuli   Did you like that son?

Abe   And I'd nod. In Brooklyn we stayed in the car … He pointed out
buildings that meant *nothing* to me.

Schmuli   That's Nachman the butcher's shop. There's Yossi Perlov's
grocery.

Abe   What was he trying to show me?? Did he know me? Did he know
I'd be drawn back there, so close I can almost touch it, that sometimes
I cross Heyward Street and just stare at the men behind the beards,
searching for what—myself?? I mean, what if I was actually *meant* to
live that life? It's not like the freedoms of this one bring me so much
pleasure. Did he know me?? That kills me, Julia. Even the possibility.
Not that it excuses my awkward fumble around wanting to see you. Of
course I can't blame you for not writing back. Has it been two months?
Three? It feels like years. But I swear I never meant to inflict any real
damage. Just to generate the kinds of small excitements that break up
routines and give a person something to look forward to. And I wasn't
gonna write this but then I figured what's the harm. Maybe I'll just keep

writing to you—years of one-sided correspondence. Isn't that really what being a novelist is, anyway?

Sophie   Can I come in?

Abe   I'm sorry. I know I said I'd be down … an hour ago.

Sophie   It's fine. Your dinner's in the fridge.

Abe   You know how people say *Orphan of Vilnius* is this masterful tale of the cost of remembering—an allegory about the way the Holocaust is just lodged in our brains.

Sophie   They have said that, yes.

Abe   So I realize that for me the book just tells this small story. About this classical violinist—

Sophie   Isaac. The violinist of Vilnius. Try saying that three times fast.

Abe   Come on, Sophie I'm working through something …

Sophie   Sorry, go on.

Abe   So yeah, his whole family is murdered before his eyes and what does he do to stop it? Nothing.

Sophie (*really asking*)   What could he have done?

Abe   And after the war, all he wants is to play the violin and he's absurdly talented; they want him at Carnegie Hall, at the Musikverein in Vienna, in London at Royal Albert Hall; and so he wanders the world for years, but he can't find God in any of those great halls and he can't grow up; he can't be anyone in the absence of his parents. He has no one to play for.

Sophie   I know you don't think so, but you're gonna be okay. You really will, you …

Abe (*quietly*)   That's what they said after my mother died.

Sophie   And haven't you been. More or less.

Abe   No. Never. Never okay.

… I know that sounds … ungrateful. But you know what I mean. You know it's not about you, or the kids.

Sophie I know that. And they know that … But they miss you … Robby keeps asking when you two are gonna finish *Winnie the Pooh*. He won't read it on his own. He's *waiting* for you …

Abe *looks down, ashamed. Beat.*

Sophie You're not your father, Abe. You're here.

Abe Hineni. Here I am.

A breath. And then we're interrupted by **Esther***'s cries/screams.*

Esther Where are they?

Schmuli, where are they?

Schmuli Esther, please calm down.

CHAPTER SIX (Or, Destruction)

Esther Where are my girls, Schmuli, you tell me this instant.

Schmuli They're just fine. Don't worry.

Esther Don't worry? Their closets are emptied. Their things are gone. Even their beds are stripped. So don't tell me they're okay; tell me where they are.

Schmuli I can't do that.

Esther Yes you can. And you will. Right now.

Nothing.

Right now!!

Nothing.

Okay I will beg you. Schmuli tell me, please please tell me.

She gets down on her knees.

Schmuli!

Schmuli Esther just … Please.

Esther Your father did this.

Schmuli   No.

Esther   Your father's men then. Enforcers. And this way he can stand off to the side, holier than thou.

Schmuli   It's not like that.

Esther   No? Then you tell me what it's like.

Beat.

Tell me, Schmuli, or I will go crazy. I will scream in the streets. I will be very immodest.

Schmuli   But don't you see that that is where this has come from!? That you have brought this on yourself.

Esther   What?

Schmuli   All the books. And the radio. And the going outside without your stockings.

Esther   That was one time! I was pregnant in August. It was too hot!

Schmuli   And this talk of a pill to stop having children.

Esther   That was a private conversation. That was between you and me. Did your father find out about that?

Schmuli   I was curious if he'd heard of such a thing.

Esther   … Oh Schmuli. No.

Schmuli   He is the person in our community to whom one goes about such things.

Esther   You fool. You dumbkopf.

Schmuli   You can't speak that way to me, Esther! I am your husband!

Esther   Then get our girls back. Get them back. Right now.

Schmuli   It's not that simple.

Esther   Where are they? I'll go and get them. I'll strap Abraham to my chest and bang down the door.

Schmuli   You are not to see them.

Beat.

Esther   For how long.

Beat.

No. No no no no no.

My babies, Schmuli.

Schmuli   Esther.

Esther (*suddenly calm*)   You see, I do the physical therapies with Leah every night for her limp.

I prepare Miriam her own dinner because she cannot tolerate any salt.

I read them to sleep otherwise they are afraid the goyim will kidnap them when the light is out.

They need me. I am their mother.

Schmuli   You should not have said that to me, about not wanting more children.

Esther   You khazer, I didn't mean take away the children
I already have!!

Schmuli   Don't say things you can't take back.

Esther (*dryly*)   And Abraham? He is only still here because he was in the hospital with me, being born?

Schmuli   He will join his sisters, as I understand it.

Esther   No. We're leaving.

Schmuli   You can't leave.

Esther   I am. I am taking Abraham and you can't stop me.

Schmuli   Don't be impulsive. You leave and you can never return. You will bring even more shame on the family.

Esther   What choice have you left me?? To stay here and try in vain to get a glimpse of my children as they are picked up from yeshiva? To continue to live in your house and submit to the "mitzvah" with the man who stole away the only joy in my life? I cannot do it. I will not. No ... You have not seen me from the moment we met. Not even once. If you had, you would not have allowed this to happen. This ... destruction.

Schmuli   There was no stopping it, Esther. Once it started.

Esther   That is what a nebech says to justify his actions. A weak, weak man.

Schmuli   I am not weak!! I mean, isn't it possible that I might agree? That even I felt you were taking things too far??

Esther   No you're just scared. Admit it.

Schmuli   I am! I *am* scared. I have a wife bent on tearing down the very walls that are keeping us safe!

Esther   All an illusion. There are no walls.

Schmuli (*unbroken and emotional*)   There are. And they're *here*. Out there, you're vulnerable—to everything. And you'll become just like everyone else. Succumbing to the petty temptations that destroy men's souls.

Esther   … Oh, Schmuli. We are already just like everyone else. Can't you see that?

The lights shift.

Julia   I'm sorry, Abe. For the long silence. And that you've been … struggling. It's not an excuse but I was on location for three months in Australia. My family was with me, and even though he and I barely saw each other, when I'd get home from the set there James would be, waiting for me, a glass of wine at the ready, like this eager, patient puppy. I felt terrible about it. So I hope you understand why I couldn't write to you, even though I wanted to.

Abe   Julia, reading your email was like hearing my name called while walking down a street in a foreign country where I didn't think anyone knew me. Or to be more physiological about it, I got tingles. Goose bumps. Why? Because—miracle of miracles!—not only did you suddenly reappear, but what a gift to know that our correspondence makes you feel guilty. Because if it makes you feel guilty there is something illicit about it, and if there's something illicit about it … Well, you get the gist. Please forgive my rejoicing at the good working order of your conscience. Not that I think we have anything to be ashamed of. We're just two adults approaching middle age with access to Wi-Fi who derive some small satisfaction from seeing what words the other one has to say.

Also, I think you're beautiful—luminous, even. But that goes without saying. When it comes to you.

Julia   Don't you wish you had a not very good working knowledge of a foreign language? I think it would be something not to know exactly what you're saying, or what others are saying to you. Sometimes I think we understand too clearly, you know?

Abe   Okay ... so you didn't respond to my manifesto in celebration of your guilt.

Julia   I will admit there is a certain rush that comes along with getting an intimate look into someone else's life that you really have no right to. I think that's the source of any guilt, if it existed. And maybe we can leave it at that?

Abe   Quite right. And very sensible. A look into someone's life. Yes. But not just anyone's—someone whose work could bring chills, and who seemed to be speaking directly to you from faraway.

Yesterday I was reading the Class Notes section of my college's alumni magazine where the secretary of the oldest class made a plea to classmates now well into their nineties to write in with news. "So much is still left unsaid" he wrote—which struck me. After all those years what could still be unsaid, unspoken?

And I found myself writing an entry about my life now, full of things best left unsaid: *Abraham Hausman, father of two, husband of one, lives and works in Brooklyn New York, which, if it weren't so nice, wouldn't be worth the embarrassing cliché. He writes books that touch on the American Jewish experience but were met with a shrug by both parents, dismissed as too Jewish by his mother and not Jewish enough by his father. Also his mother, who for the first part of her life found refuge in books, came to hate them for painting a world she finally entered but didn't recognize. So no wonder the writing, at first joyful, now feels like hard labor, the slightest cold parking Abe in front of the TV for hours, days even. His children bring him unquantifiable amounts of delight, and also fear, irritation, concern. Once his daughter asked whether, in a* Sophie's Choice-*type situation, she should pick her mother or father to live. Not only was this troubling in terms of the temperament and preoccupations of the questioner—but Abe didn't have an easy answer. Of course he should say she should choose his wife. But the truth was that Abe felt _he_ would be better equipped to be alone. And, despite almost nauseating guilt, that maybe he would enjoy moving on. So he stayed silent. A reticence in life matched, perhaps, by verbosity on the page, an outlet Abe wonders if his quiet father could have used. Sometimes Abe wonders if his father would still be alive if he hadn't been lonely, one black hat in a sea of hats. Tales of his father's weakness persuade Abe that weakness lives in him too. In fact, he can sometimes be found practically luxuriating in it, most recently in the permission he's granted himself to fall in love with a movie star. And no—it's not what you're thinking. It's not just from an innocent distance ... It's the real deal, the kind of connection you're lucky to find once in your life, if ever.*

Anyway! Fellow alums, if you're ever in Brooklyn, give Abe a shout! Though chances are he doesn't really want to see you, or he'd have been in touch himself.

Beat.

Julia   I don't really know what to say. You've put me in an awkward position. I can't have you being in love with me.

Abe   Can you have me some other way then? I would just love to be had by you.

Sophie *enters.*

Sophie (*angrily*)   Abe, can I talk to you?

Abe   Right now?

Sophie   Yeah, right now!

Abe   Okay.

Sophie   Okay.

Abe   Okay.

It's as though now she doesn't know what to say.

Sophie   Actually ... it can wait.

Abe (*truly asking*)   What's going on with you.

Sophie   What's going on with me??

Abe   Yeah.

Sophie   I don't know. You seem to think you have this monopoly on confusion—

Abe   I probably do think that, yeah.

Sophie   And I know—I know—I have these two living parents and so I'm very lucky but I think because of all your, your ...

Abe   Tragedy, heartache, trauma.

Sophie   Yeah, because of all that—we don't ever focus on ...

Abe   You.

Sophie   Right! Like yesterday? I was picking Esther up from school
and again—again—someone mistakes me for a … I mean, the babysitter
of this boy who's having a total meltdown, like he's literally tearing his
clothes off *outside*—the babysitter, who's Black, turns to me and gives
me this look like "they don't pay me enough for this shit" and then says,
"maybe I can switch with you?" because Esther is well-behaved … at
least in public.

Abe   That doesn't mean that she—

Sophie   Trust me. But it's not that it happened, that it happens; it's
how it makes me feel. Why on earth should it bother me so much?
What am I so afraid of? And the other day my mother calls and she says
she's thought about it and she doesn't like that you're sending the kids
to Hebrew School; she says the Jews ostracized her and Dad and that
it's an insult to my father to send them. And I'm like "is that what *Dad*
thinks?"—a seventy-five-year-old man from Mississippi who couldn't
care less what the Jews think, and she says "yes even if he would never
admit it." Which is … I mean, she will never acknowledge how crazy
she is, probably because crazy people don't know they're crazy, but it's
insane because it's not like I'm not … Jewish too. Ish. Maybe I'd like to
send my kids to Hebrew School too!

Abe   Do you?

Sophie   No! But it's the principle. About how much she should intervene
in our lives. And yeah, if my own work was … going better this other
stuff might not matter so much but now it's … I mean, the problem is
probably that I don't want to be any of the things that I actually am …

Abe (*not a dismissal; he's really trying*)   It sounds like you could use a
drink, Soph.

Sophie   I could use a vacation.

Like maybe we should go somewhere and just … unplug.

Don't you think just getting away maybe? The two of us.

Abe   Maybe.

But I'm not sure I need to unplug.

Sophie   Well I do.

Abe   We'll do it soon.

Sophie   When?

Abe   Soon.

Beat.

Sophie   Okay I know you hate hearing my dreams—

Abe   When did I say that?

Sophie   It's the look on your face when I start to tell one. But last night I had this … Well, I dreamed an animal got into our house and disrupted it. Like you'd go into rooms and things weren't in the right places.

Abe   That sounds less like an animal than just the way we live.

Sophie   Well then I went into the kids' room and they were sleeping, peacefully. Until I got closer and found that they'd been mauled in their beds.

Abe   God, Sophie.

Sophie   I know.

Abe   Don't have that dream again. Please.

Sophie   And when I woke up, you were gone.

Abe   I couldn't sleep so I went for a run.

Beat.

Sophie (*quietly*)   No … that's not what I meant.

CHAPTER SEVEN (or, The Visit)

Schmuli *appears on* **Esther**'s *doorstep. They stand facing each other. Neither knows what to say. It has been four years.*

Esther What are you doing here?

Schmuli How are you, Esther?

Esther Fine.

Schmuli Oh good! I'm very well too.

Esther So we are all doing well then.

Schmuli And this is your place. It's, um. Well. It's … Are there any windows?

Esther Like where *we* were living was such a palace. Rivka will be down soon. She comes at 9 to watch *Face the Nation*, so.

Schmuli Where is Abraham? Is he home?

Esther Where are my *girls*? Did you bring them?

Silence. **Schmuli** *is fiddling with his hat.*

Oh just take it off already, Schmuli. Please.

Schmuli It's something, Esther. To see you like this. I mean, your hair; it's …

Instinctively she reaches to cover it, realizing he's never seen her like this.

Schmuli (*with so much feeling*) No, it's beautiful.

She is moved, and confused.

Esther (*this is all too much for her*) I have to go. I'm sorry.

Schmuli No, wait. Please wait. You think I didn't see you all those years. But I did. I saw you. I saw you when you ate something you disliked but tried to hide the unpleasantness. I heard you murmur in your sleep, asking always for your mother. I saw the way you looked at me, the way you look at me still, which is not with disgust, but with wistfulness, as though things could be different. With the affectionate frustration one reserves for one's children. You can't see yourself. I am telling you the look on your face.

Esther The look on my face.

Schmuli   It's been years. I think you could be forgiven. I think I can forgive you.

Esther   What makes you think *I* could ever forgive *you*??

Schmuli   Are you happy here, Esther?

Esther   Abraham is a very bright boy. He excels in school. Already.

Schmuli   I brought him a present.

Esther   Why?

Schmuli (*with real emotion*)   It's his birthday today, nu? Don't you understand why I'm here? It's been long enough. Four years, Esther. I miss my son. I feel him like this gaping hole in my …

He hands **Esther** *a wrapped present.*

Will you give it to him?

Esther (*drily*)   What is it? The Gemara?

Schmuli   *The Collected Stories of Winnie the Pooh.*

Esther   Oh.

Schmuli   I read it. It is a story a father tells his son.

Esther   I don't know what to say.

Schmuli   Life isn't the same without you. Home isn't the same without you.

Esther (*quietly, reflective*)   … I dream about it, you know. The way you wake up on Fridays and the air feels different. Everything closed by noon and the women scurrying for challah, for fish, for wine. The flurry of hats and coats on Marcy Avenue, rushing to be home before dark. And the birthdays and the holidays … and the way no one is forgotten. Everyone suspended together over all the years that have passed and all the years to come in a song that will never end.

Schmuli   … I knew you'd be trouble from the moment I agreed to marry you. You'd rejected all those matches, good men too: Schlomo Lipsky, Chezky Blankenstok, Dovid Mendelbaum.

Esther   You knew about that?

Schmuli   It's what clinched it for me, why I had to have you. And why I need you still. See, I will not remarry. You are my bashert. The only one for me. A woman with her own mind. A skeptic.

Esther (*quietly*)   But that's the thing. I don't think my mind works right, Schmuli.

Schmuli   Why do you say that?

Esther   I thought when I got out of Brooklyn, it would be as though the bars had lifted. But it turns out they are inside me. That I am looking for life to give me something it will never provide.

Schmuli   Which is what?

Esther   That's the problem. I'm not sure.

Schmuli   Oh my liebling. Come home now. It's not like I have it all figured out. It's not like I don't have doubts.

Esther   So, what. You are suggesting we just … change nothing? And I simply come back with you?

Schmuli   Is this not a change? It is your choice.

(*With real feeling.*)

I have … given over to you.

Back to **Abe** *and* **Julia**, *instant messaging.*

Julia   Do you ever think, if you had it all to do over again, you'd undo anything?

Abe   Anything? I'd undo everything.

Julia   No you wouldn't.

Abe   I would. I thought you would know that about me, by now.

Julia   I don't even think I really know my own *husband*. Isn't that insane?

Abe   Sometimes, when I've been out all day, I get home and Sophie literally has her hands over her ears. I'm not sure if she's shutting me out, or the kids. Or both.

Julia   Sometimes it gets to be too much. You imagine living other lives.

Abe (*matter-of-fact*)   That's called being a person, Julia.

Julia   I think maybe knowing you has made me sadder than I was.

Abe (*chuckling*)   You're not the first woman to have said that to me.

Julia   Does Sophie … is she happier than you are?

Abe   Well that's a pretty low bar. So yes—even if she's been a little distracted lately. And by lately I mean the last decade or so. But I can't expect her to be enchanted by me forever. Really she's been generous. She hasn't gotten all the things she wanted.

Julia   She sounds wonderful, and patient.

Abe   She hasn't left me yet.

Julia   I feel that way about James. Like why hasn't he fled so many times?

Abe   Do you want your marriage upended?

Julia   Why, should we run off together?

Long beat.

Abe   I don't know. Probably.

Beat.

But then we'd be in the less than ideal position of having to trust someone who just proved him or herself patently untrustworthy.

Also there *are* the children to think of.

Which makes me sound like a character in a Russian novel.

Julia (*surprised*)   You've really thought about this.

Abe   Sometimes Sophie talks about having another baby.

Julia   Well … it's not for the faint of heart. And I say that as someone whose babies both routinely required three people to change their diapers. So vast was the mess. It would hit the walls, Abe.

Abe   Also, all I can think about sometimes is having a baby with you.

Julia (*quietly*)   You do?

Abe   What he would look like. That we would name him after my father. His artistic pedigree that would send him right into the sciences … That our lives would be officially intertwined. That it would be awfully fun to make a baby with you.

Julia (*impulsive, out of nowhere*)   Abe, do you prefer me to your wife?

Beat.

Abe   Well, that's a deeply unfair question.

Julia   Is it?

Abe   There's so much I don't know about you. Whereas I've known Sophie forever. She's practically an extension of me.

Julia   You really think you know everything about her?

Abe   More or less.

Julia   Do you think she knows everything about you?

Abe   She's seen me through so much. So yes. But are there things I keep from her? ... Sure.

Julia   Such as.

Abe   Oh, I don't know ... Probably the same things I keep from myself.

Julia   What do you keep from yourself. You can tell me.

Beat.

Abe   I'll set a scene for you: 7th grade. My mother was having terrible nightmares about my grandfather coming to kidnap me. The dreams were so bad we kept all the lights on, in every room, at all times. But on this particular day, when I got home from basketball practice I found my mother sitting completely still on the couch in total darkness. I went up to her, "are you ok, Mameh," And out of the darkness, her voice, and I remember it as being filled with an almost childlike wonder, said: "Abraham I've just realized that you are my only reason for being alive." And then she said it again ... year after year after year after year. Until, at a certain point, I guess I stopped being a good enough reason.

Julia   You think you disappointed your mother, don't you. Let her down. You'll never let that go.

Abe   No I disappointed my *father*. When I was an adult I ignored virtually all of his attempts to get in touch, or to see me. And all he'd ever wanted was a son. So yeah, him I let down. I *killed* my mother.

Julia   No you didn't, Abe.

Abe   You're a nice person, Julia, and you say nice things. But when a person exterminates herself, there's an inescapable truth at the center of it all.

Julia   Which is.

Abe   They could have been saved.

Julia   That's just not always true.

Abe   It's incontrovertibly true. If someone else hadn't been selfish, they could have been saved …

I'll explain: I was on my book tour in San Diego, for *Orphan*—which is of course richly ironic.

Julia   Why is that ironic?

Abe   Because I spent years of my life, Julia, years when my parents were both *alive*, toiling over this book about a fucking *orphan*.

Julia   Don't do that to yourself. You didn't know what was coming.

Abe   So there I am standing in front of Barnes and Noble, having just read from that stupid book, when my mother calls and says, I need you to come home, Abraham. My sister Leah had just had her third baby and my mother was desperate to be there. Each baby my sisters had was another huge blow, each one a reminder of everything my mother didn't have. But I was a week away from the end of the tour. And this wasn't the first time she'd asked this of me. So I told her she would have to wait. I said one week, Mameh. And I hung up.

Julia   You've never told me this part of the story.

Abe   Sophie doesn't even know it. How could I tell her? You see, my mother begged me to marry her. For years, she *begged* me. She loved Sophie like she was her own daughter and my mother was tragically short on family for someone who so badly wanted it. She was unsubtle about it. (*With a slight Yiddish lilt:*) "Abraham, you're going to marry that girl; you want to even if you don't know it yet." She was a Jewish mother, whether she liked it or not. She was also my mother. My only mother.

Beat.

I got the call when I was on the train, somewhere between San Diego and LA. My phone buzzed in my pocket and I knew. I did. I knew. So I didn't pick up. This was one of the many times I didn't answer when my father called.

I flew home. I took a cab from the airport straight to Williamsburg, straight to Sophie. It was the middle of the night. I walked up those five flights of stairs and banged on the door until she let me in. And she let me in because I let her believe I was who she wanted me to be. She let me in because she was genuinely in love with me, which is actually the hardest thing to ... But how could I not be with her? How could I not have those children my mother so desperately wanted? Every book I ever write will be a mea culpa. Every word a reminder of that particular cruelty. No, *everything* is a reminder. The days I spend in front of blank screens when I should be ... I mean, my kids are growing so fast I hardly recognize them. And I just ... I don't want anyone else to die. Please. Don't let anyone else ... I can't do it. I can't tell my wife I didn't love her the way she loved me, that I *submitted* to our marriage. I don't even want to believe it. Could there be anything sadder? But the saddest things are usually true. My mother in the darkness. The way when I look at my wife I feel such shame. You understand now.

Silence. Then we see **Julia** *exit.*

Julia? Are you there?

Julia??

Sophie *appears in the doorway.*

Sophie   Oh I'm here all right.

Abe (*quietly*)   What's going on.

Sophie   What's going on is that you just said you never loved me.

Abe   I don't ... What do you ... Wait.

Sophie   Why would you say that, Abe? I mean, you do love me. I know you do.

Abe   Of course I love you. What's going on?

Sophie (*dawning on her*)   Or maybe you don't. Maybe you really don't. And never did. Maybe you literally never loved me.

Then, really hitting her.

Oh my god.

Abe   Soph, Sophie ... where is this all coming from? I'm not quite ...

Sophie   I feel like such a ... I just thought it was a game. I don't know why I thought it was a game. I mean: "Reading your email was like hearing my name called while walking down a street in a foreign country where I didn't think anyone knew me."

Beat.

Abe   Please Sophie. I don't understand.

Sophie   And you don't know me at all, Abe.

The way you describe me. A little patient woman. Poor Sophie. Who doesn't like being such a failure but tolerates it because what else can you do.

Abe   I never said that.

Sophie   You said worse.

Abe   I'm just … I'm … I can't wrap my head around …

Sophie   The night of that reading. You couldn't stop talking about how she was there. Julia Cheever. Could I believe it? Like seeing a beloved character in real life. It messes with your equilibrium. Your sense of what's real and not real.

Abe   I still can't believe she came to that reading. I still can't believe that she wrote me. That she kept writing to me.

Sophie   But she never wrote to you, Abe. Not even once.

Beat.

Abe   Not even once.

Sophie   That night … the night of the reading … I saw something in you I hadn't seen in a long time. It took me awhile to realize what it was, but then I did: how much you wanted to impress her. And I saw how little you care about impressing me. Not that I can blame you. It's old hat, impressing me. But I wanted to know what that felt like—not to feel wanted by you, though there is that, of course, but to feel worthy of your making an effort. So I'll admit: it started off as a little joke because you were just SO bowled over to have seen her that night. You couldn't stop talking about it. But then you got so into it. And I got so into it.

Abe   God. Sophie.

Sophie   And I got this little taste of what it must be to feel important. To feel like a success in the world. It's heady.

Abe   Please no. Anything but this.

Sophie   Anything but this. I agree.

Abe (*dawning on him*)   Hundreds—no thousands—of messages. Every single one a lie.

Sophie   And you don't think you were lying to me?

Abe   I *was* lying to you. But in a less fucked up way.

Sophie   I would dispute that.

Abe   You deliberately set this trap for me.

Sophie   It was sort of like dating you again. It was addictive. But then you sold out our marriage so completely for this fantasy—

Abe   You wanted me to! For some sick reason you wanted me to!

Sophie   You said you wanted to have a baby with this woman! A baby, Abe. Can you imagine how that would sound to me? When you've made *me* feel like an asshole for even bringing it up.

Abe   I can't imagine any of this. It is literally unimaginable to me.

Sophie   How long would you have let it go on for? Forever?

Abe   I don't know. Maybe! But you tricked me. You manipulated me. You got me to say exactly what you wanted me to say.

Sophie   That your dead mother forced you to marry me? That you never loved me? That's what I wanted to hear??

Abe   You wanted me to see things I didn't wanna see. And then I did. I *saw* them. And now here we are.

I mean, you let her console me after my father died!

Sophie   Well, you didn't want *me* to!! And it seemed to help.

Abe   Help?! It was a fiction, Sophie. All a fiction! Why would you do this? Why would you push me into this woman's arms?

Sophie   It didn't take much pushing.

Abe (*realizing*)   You enjoyed it, didn't you … You fucking enjoyed it!

Sophie   I just thought it would become obvious to you at some point. And it never did.

Abe   You're a good writer, Sophie.

Sophie   I don't think I enjoyed it. I got stomachaches. Sometimes I felt like I couldn't breathe.

Abe   So you knew how wrong it was. See? You knew.

Sophie   And so did you, Abe. You knew too.

Beat.

Abe (*this is impossibly sad*)   This is … I mean, Sophie. Everything about this.

Sophie (*this is unbearable too*)   I wish you could have come to me about your mom's … I mean, I *am* sorry that you feel so responsible for her, um … I don't think you should.

Abe   But I did go to you. I went right to you. Right to your doorstep. And you took me in.

Sophie   I did.

Abe (*begging her not to*)   You can't leave me over this. You wouldn't. I mean, what I did was terrible; it was undeniably wrong but if I was having an affair, or something like an affair, wasn't it … with you?

Sophie   … Was it? I don't know what I know anymore. But I don't buy that our marriage was arranged, Abe. I really don't. We chose each other. … I think what we're seeing now is that it wasn't the right choice.

CHAPTER EIGHT (or, Fiction)

Lights shift. **Schmuli** *is outside in the snow;* **Esther** *is in the doorway, between worlds.*

Schmuli   Esther!

Esther!

Come out here!

It's delicious.

It's beautiful.

It's bracing.

Just look into the sky.

Esther   Oh Schmuli, it's too cold. I'll stay here.

Schmuli   No, you have to come. Come on mommellah.

It's nice. It makes you feel alive.

And for once I don't feel too warm.

For once I'm not shvitzing.

Esther *starts to go to him.*

That's right, Esther. "Come to me."

She smiles, despite herself.

Esther   I'm not sure I like it.

I need boots.

I feel the wet in my socks.

Schmuli   If it is unpleasant it will make the warming up later all the sweeter.

Esther   Who died and made you a philosopher, Schmuli Simcha.

Schmuli   No one has died, my love.

No one will die.

A pause. A breath. **Abe** *enters. We are online. At least a year later.*

Abe   Julia?

Are you there?

Are you there, Julia?

Sophie *enters*.

Oh there you are.

Julia Cheever, right?

This is Tom Brokaw.

It's nice to meet you.

Beat.

Sophie (*playing along but wary*)   Tom. Can it really be you?

Abe   It's me. I came straight from speaking at a convention of members of the greatest generation. They were all dead so it didn't take long.

Sophie   So no stage fright.

Abe   You'd think, but actually it was brutal. The dead really are very judgmental.

Sophie   So … what are you doing here.

Abe   I came looking for you.

Sophie   Abe.

Abe   Tom.

Sophie   Fine. Tom.

Abe   I've always thought you were so cute. If I didn't have such a wonderful, supportive family in the heart of the Midwest I might lie down at your feet.

Sophie   Okay I'm not sure where the fantasy ends and the reality begins here.

Abe   Isn't that always true.

Sophie   How are you, Abe?

Abe   Oh about as well as an orphaned soon to be divorcee with children suddenly old enough to walk themselves to school can be expected to be. Why we didn't have another kid when we had the chance I'll never know.

Sophie   Are you joking? I can't tell if you're joking.

Abe Of course it's possible that we've made a real mess of the ones we already have.

Sophie Well, Robby was assigned a book report this week—he could write about anything—the Yankees, polar bears, anything—and he's writing it on *Schindler's List*, so yeah: maybe.

Abe Yup, irretrievably ruined.

Sophie You know, I actually think they're doing okay, considering.

Abe That should be my epitaph: He did okay, considering.

Or the title of my new book.

Which I finished, by the way. I hoped I could share it with you.

Sophie Oh I don't know, Abe.

Abe "I don't know, Abe; you're awesome—and actually I really do think I'd like to read it."

Sophie Ha ha.

Abe It's not what you think … I don't even know if it's for … general consumption. I really just want to show it to you.

Sophie Only me.

Abe It's about my parents.

Sophie Okay.

Abe All I can think of is my father dying alone. The snow in his beard, and no one beside him. I can't get that image … I couldn't have it end that way.

Sophie So you rewrote the ending?

Abe Now they end up together. In Albany, in the depths of winter. At that house on Amy Lane, with the always broken front porch light. Only now my father has fixed it.

Sophie Did it make you feel better?

Abe It feels as real to me as if it truly happened.

Isn't that odd?

Sophie No I don't think so.

Abe   So you'll read it?

Sophie   … I'm not sure. I'll think about it.

Abe   Thank you for thinking about it.

Sophie   You know I finished my book too.

Abe   Sophie, that's amazing.

Sophie   It is. And I think it's really good.

Abe   There is no doubt in my mind.

Sophie   There is, but that's okay. It doesn't matter. It's about me. Us. It's memoir-*ish*.

Abe   What's it called?

Sophie   The Wanderers, maybe.

Abe   I like it. The Jews in the desert for forty years.

Sophie   Sort of. Or just the idea of it. That it can take a lifetime just to grow up. To let go of a certain sort of galvanizing restlessness that leaves you always empty.

Happy birthday by the way. Belatedly.

Abe   Thank you. Though "happy" doesn't really apply at a certain point, does it?

Sophie   I think it can. I think it should. For our whole lives, it should.

Abe *is at a loss.*

Abe   Do you wanna know how I spent it, my birthday? It's kinda crazy. You won't believe it.

Sophie   Try me.

Abe   So I was at this Rockefeller Foundation gala.

Sophie   Okay, this is really stretching my disbelief.

Abe   No, wait. It was in London. A special anniversary event.

Beat.

Sophie   In London. How'd you get there?

Abe   I flew.

Sophie   And you weren't scared?

Abe   I was terrified. But I guess I put my faith in God, or something like God.

Sophie   Really?

Abe   And as the plane rose into the sky, I prayed. Mostly for forgiveness. *Avinu Malkeinu.* Hear our voice. *Avinu Malkeinu.* Have compassion on us, on our parents and on our children. *Avinu Malkeinu.* Inscribe us for blessing in the book of life.

And then I emerged from the plane and found my way into that beautiful city where holiday lights hung in every window and the snow-covered sidewalks were illuminated by streetlamps like it could have been two hundred years ago and I was filled with this ... ecstasy I guess.

Sophie (*genuine*)   Wow. Good for you.

Abe   And at the gala, there were readings. Alice Munro. Ian McEwan. Toni Morrison. And then Philip Roth's up there and he reads a little excerpt from *Portnoy.*

Sophie   No shit.

Abe   And who do you think is in the front row but ...

Sophie (*quietly*)   Julia Cheever.

Abe   Ding ding ding. And after Roth reads, she raises her hand and asks how he would characterize himself—is he Jewish first, or a man, or an American. Or an asshole ... Or an artist.

Sophie   What did he say.

Abe   He said ... There is nothing I could say that would not be a fiction except that I am first and last the product of my parents.

Sophie   Huh.

Abe   And after the reading she sees me.

Sophie   Was it because you were standing two feet away staring at her?

Abe   Hilarious Sophie. No, I wasn't. But she literally came up to me and was like:

Julia *enters.*

Julia   Is that Abraham Hausman?

Abe   That is.

Julia　This is so funny.

Abe　Is it?

Julia　I've been hoping to meet you. You gave a reading a few years back at Book Court—in Brooklyn.

Abe　You were there. In the front row. I remember.

Julia　Wow. I wondered if you'd seen me. Not to be immodest or anything.

Abe　No, be immodest. If I were you I'd be immodest too.

Julia　Well I just wanted to let you know I'm a big fan.

Abe　As I am of yours.

Julia　I think your writing is sort of … luminous.

Abe　I don't know what to say.

Julia　What are you working on these days?

Abe　Oh just, basically, trying to heal the gaping chasm in my marriage and my life that my wife pretending to be you writing to me for a year and a half created.

Back to **Sophie**.

And did she laugh.

Sophie　You didn't really say that to her.

Abe　I did.

Sophie　… You really are something, Tom Brokaw.

Abe　I know. That's just how we roll in the not quite greatest generation.

And then—get this—she told me she'd like to be in touch. Maybe she could pitch *A Theory of Milk* around LA, get a "long-overdue"—her words—adaptation underway. And I politely declined.

Sophie　You did?

Abe　Yeah.

Sophie　Well that was idiotic because we could use the money.

Abe　You're joking.

Sophie   Only half.

Abe   Not a problem. We can add it to my prodigious inventory of mistakes and accidents. From the accident of my birth all the way up to however I will manage to botch this crucial communication with my bashert … (*As open/vulnerable as he's ever been.*) The only one for me … The real deal.

Sophie *sighs.*

I can feel you sighing through the computer.

Sophie   Can you?

Abe   I can feel it all. Sophie.

Beat.

Sophie   So I had a dream last night.

Abe   Oh no, please not a repeat of the one about our children getting mauled.

Sophie   No. In this one, Robby was little again.

He sleep-walked into the living-room, where we were sitting in the bright light, and lay down on the couch next to us as though we weren't there at all. His breath moved gently through him. His palms were face up, like a little supplicant, only it wasn't clear what he wanted. Outside it was snowing, and it seemed, in that moment, like he might be small forever.

And then you scooped him up, like in a picture book, and carried him back to his room, this baby we once had, your lips pressed to his forehead the whole way.

Beat. **Abe** *is crying.*

That was it. That was my dream. Or maybe it's a memory. I'm not sure there's any difference.

Abe   I don't …
I don't have any words.

Sophie   I think that's okay. Abe.

Abe   *Ein ba'al ha-nes makir b'niso.*
Sophie.

Sophie (*gently*)   What does that mean?

Breath.

Esther   Schmuli I'm freezing my tuchus off!

Schmuli   Good!

Esther   I'm not happy.

Schmuli   That's okay. Make an angel.

Esther   What?

Schmuli   Make an angel in the snow.

And then our children will come out and lie down in the space we have made for them.

Esther   I don't know if I can.

Schmuli   Esther.

Ein ba'al ha-nes makir b'niso.

Beat.

Esther   I know.

Schmuli   Let us feel how fortunate we are.

She looks at him and then, slowly, takes his hand. The lights fade to black.

End of play

Actually

Actually was originally produced in a co-production between the Geffen Playhouse (Randall Arney, Artistic Director) and the Williamstown Theatre Festival (Mandy Greenfield, Artistic Director).

The opening night at the Geffen Playhouse was on May 10, 2017, with the following cast and creative team:

Director: Tyne Rafaeli

Cast

Tom	**Jerry MacKinnon**
Amber	**Samantha Ressler**

Stage Manager	Liz Brohm
Set Designer	Tim Mackabee
Costume Designer	Caitlin Ward
Lighting Designer	Lap Chi Chu
Sound Designer	Vincent Olivieri

The opening night at the Williamstown Theatre Festival was on August 12, 2017, with the following cast and creative team:

Director: Lileana Blain-Cruz

Cast

Tom	**Joshua Boone**
Amber	**Alexandra Socha**

Stage Manager	Dane Urban
Set Designer	Adam Rigg
Costume Designer	Paloma Young
Lighting Designer	Ben Stanton
Sound Designer	Jane Shaw

The play subsequently opened at Manhattan Theatre Club (Lynne Meadow, Artistic Director, Barry Grove Executive Producer) on November 13, 2017.

The cast was as follows:

Tom	**Joshua Boone**
Amber	**Alexandra Socha**

The play was developed/written in part at the Sallie B. Goodman Retreat at McCarter Theatre.

Characters

Amber, *early to mid-twenties, high-strung, talkative, charmingly neurotic. She does not present as insecure. She is Jewish.*

Tom, *early to mid-twenties, appealing and confident with some swagger that conceals a deeper vulnerability. He is Black.*

*Lights up on a college party. Princeton. Two students, freshmen—**Amber**
and **Tom**—are outside on the quad. A first date. Sort of. They're drinking.
A lot.*

Amber   So I was reading tonight in our psych book about the pratfall
effect, and it's actually really interesting: it's about how a person's
attractiveness increases or decreases after he or she makes a mistake. So a
highly-competent person, like, say, a celebrity, would be *more* likable after
committing a blunder, while the opposite would be true if—

Tom   God, do you ever stop talking?

Amber   What?

Tom (*with a small smile*)   Just stop talking.

Amber   Okay.

Tom   I'm gonna kiss you now.

Amber   Oh. Okay.

They do. **Amber***'s not sure what to do with her hand so it hovers awkwardly
over* **Tom***'s shoulder, not touching it.*

Amber   Let's play a game. Let's play Two Truths and a Lie.

Tom (*emphatic*)   Um. No.

Amber   Come on.

Tom   Okay. I have two truths for you … I hate games and I hate that game.

Amber   But you'll play it.

Tom   And why would I do that?

Amber (*forcing herself out of her comfort zone*)   If you wanna sleep
with me tonight, for one thing.

Tom (*without missing a beat*)   Who goes first?

A sharp shift in tone. **Amber** *and* **Tom** *abruptly turn to face the audience.*

Amber   So.

Tom (*to the audience*)   In some ways I've been on trial my entire life.

Amber It wasn't an actual trial. It was a hearing but it felt like a trial. We
sat across from each other. At these long wooden tables. I felt like I was a
character in *The Crucible*. Maybe because our "trial" was in a classroom
where I'd happened to read *The Crucible* earlier that semester.

Tom   We sat across from each other.

Amber   The room was very cold. I had to wear *two* layers. The cardigan I carry with me because I am *always* cold but also my jacket. *Inside.*

Tom   I couldn't believe how cold this girl got. She'd have goose bumps like sitting outside on a 75-degree day.

An abrupt shift back to each other, and into the scene.

Amber   Okay my first truth is: I thought I'd fall in love on my first day of college.

Tom (*that's weird*)   First day?

Amber (*she speaks very fast*)   Well, my parents did. My dad was my mom's professor in a class called History of the American South and she liked his accent and in a sort of twisted way that he was old enough to be her father and I guess he liked being able to lord it over her and probably her looks—my mom was very attractive back then—because then they were together.

Tom   That was allowed back then?

Amber   You don't even know if anything I just said was true.

Tom   Okay. Fair point.

Amber   Second one: I have never excelled at any sport.

Tom   But you're on the squash team.

Amber   Third one: I have no feelings for you whatsoever.

Tom *stares at her.*

So now you guess.

Tom   No, I know. I'm thinking.

Amber   Lay out your thought process.

Tom   Well, I'm an arrogant bastard so I think you do like me … And that shit about your parents is either too detailed to be a lie or so detailed it's the obvious lie.

Amber   Hm. Interesting.

Tom   You're on a team here so I think you've excelled at sports. And I'm way confident you're into me—

Amber So you've said.

Tom But—I'll go with the lie is about your parents.

Amber The lie was not about my parents.

Tom Then you're no good at sports.

Amber I'm no good at sports.

Tom How the hell did you get on the squash team?

Amber *Anyone* can get on the squash team.

Tom Is that right.

Amber I mean, you don't have to be great. You can be good, or just okay. It's a great way to help you get into college. Just like being Black.

Tom (*incredulous and amused*) Um. You know you can't say that. Right?

Amber But it's not a micro-aggression or anything.

Tom Cause it's like a *macro*-aggression.

Amber (*unapologetic, matter-of-fact*) Come on. Everyone has things that help them get in. I'm not saying either of us is remotely unqualified to be here.

Tom (*in disbelief*) Wow. Okay.

Amber No, I'm sure you're super smart. You had to beat out a shit ton of other Black kids to get in. I just had to beat out some other mediocre squash players.

Tom You think my only competition was other Black kids?

Amber Mainly, yeah. We all fill some stupid niche, which reduces us to something much less than what we are, but that's the way it goes. Has it been very hard for you, being Black?

Tom (*laughing*) God, you really are, like … a piece of work.

Amber But has it?

Another sharp turn out to the audience.

Amber See it became, almost immediately, "the matter of Anthony dash Cohen." (*Bashfully.*) Which I couldn't help thinking looked like what our last name would be if we got married …

Tom   I get an email from the Office of the Vice Provost of Institutional Equity and Diversity. It's from some dude named Leslie. He made it clear that he was a dude by saying "because the name can be ambiguous I want to make you aware that I am a man." I'm told to come into the office at my very earliest convenience.

Amber (*back to the audience*)   What happened was I told Heather who told our RA Olivia who told whoever she told.

Tom   I honestly thought maybe this was about my being an asshole for not joining the Black Student Union.

Amber   But I didn't know Heather would tell anyone. She just came into my room and was like "Amber. People are saying you were *topless* at Cap last night. What the fuck. Were you super wasted?" And I'm like "that's the least of it. I mean, Thomas Anthony practically raped me." ... And she looked at me with these wide eyes, like she was kind of seeing me for the first time ... and I knew immediately that I'd said something I couldn't take back.

Tom (*back to the audience*)   So I'm sitting across from Leslie, and the guy has an enormous beard. Part of me wonders if maybe there *is* a woman behind there.

Amber   And so I tell her what happened. Or what I can remember. But I don't tell Heather everything. I mean, why should *Heather* know everything?

Tom   And he's like "I assume you know why you're here" and I'm like "enlighten me, Leslie" not realizing I shouldn't be, like, a dick right now. And he squints his eyes at me like he can't believe what he's hearing.

Okay, so even though my mom was always like "don't give anyone any reason to write you off" I'm still not great at gauging when I really should be polite. Like in 11th grade I once said to the school psychologist: "who's *your* shrink, shrink?"

I mean, I had this one weird thing and my high school sent me into therapy. What's that all about?

Amber   So I just say to Heather that things went pretty far and she's like but that's not rape and I'm like I know that Heather. What might have maybe constituted something approaching sex without my one hundred percent consent was that he got a tiny bit rough with me and at first I was into it but then I wasn't into it anymore and I stood up and was like "actually, um" but he pulled me back and kept going. And then she says, all horrified, "and all you said was 'actually'?" and I'm like yeah. And she's like "but that's not no" and I'm like I know that, Heather—I am aware that two different words in the English language are not the same word … Also, I was just so so drunk.

Abrupt shift back to the scene.

Tom   Okay, so I guess I'll say … in the spirit of truth …

Amber   Or maybe a lie.

Tom   If I can, one day I'd like to play piano professionally. Like in a symphony. Or jazz piano. Or, like, the orchestra pit of *Hamilton* / or something.

Amber   Oh god I love that show.

Tom (*impressed*)   You saw it??

Amber   No!!

Tom   Okay … The second one is … my mom is the love of my life.

Amber   Aw. That's sweet. That better not be a lie or you're kind of deranged.

Tom   The third one is …

Beat.

I feel most out of place when people would assume I feel most comfortable.

Amber   Like when?

Tom   You don't even know if that one's true.

Amber (*kind, knowing*)   I know it's true … The question is which of the other two is the lie.

Tom   Oh fuck.

Amber   What.

Tom   I fucked it up.

Amber   You forgot to lie.

Tom   I straight up told you I hate games.

Amber   Wanna do it over?

Tom   I'm just too honest. What can I say?

Amber (*gentle*)   Then tell me some other things that are true.

Beat.

Tom (*to the audience*)   I was playing the piano in one of the music rooms during a free period.

And this teacher Emily Mackey, who couldn't be more than five feet tall, and who teaches percussion, (which is like "percussion"—who even takes that?), she walks in and asks if I'd mind if she listened to me play.

I was like sure, be my guest, and I just kept playing. And yeah, maybe I stepped it up a little because I had an audience. And maybe it wasn't totally lost on me that Ms. Mackey looked about eighteen and also that she was a type I hadn't tried before—you know: boy body, flat-chested, short hair.

Amber   But, like, who is Heather to judge because she's probably always had great sex. I bet even her first time was amazing, with, like, candles, and some guy who *worshipped* her because she probably gives head like a porn star, and I'm sure she lost her virginity in, like, 9th grade so she never had to be embarrassed, in high school, that she hadn't done it.

Tom   So when she stood up and was like leaning on the piano while I played, I might've gotten pretty fancy with my fingers, just sort of dancing them over the keys.

I don't mean to come off, like … but at the time I felt I knew a coupla things. One was that I was decent-looking. Or maybe a little better than that. And the other was that I was a damn good piano player.

And she's sort of swaying. Ms. Mackey. I'm playing Bartok's third piano concerto, which is kind of a weird one, sort of all over the place, and not always the most, like, melodious, but she's *into* it.

And then, at the end of the first movement, she sits on the bench next to me so our legs are touching. And it's this fucking electric electricity and I don't know what to do about it. So I look her in the eyes and wait a second to be sure I'm reading everything right before I kiss her.

Amber   Whereas I was always really scared of *everything* about it. Like when I was little I remember wondering, like how you possibly get yourself into the situation where sex would actually occur. It all seemed so impossible to me, and embarrassing. And then, when you're older, you start thinking about how to *avoid* sex—because it's actually right there in front of you from 7th grade on, and that's, like terrifying. But no one *admits* that. No one admits that if you hook up with a guy but you don't go as far as he'd like, or if you go *too* far, like my friend Rachel did, then you end up on a private blog that does *not* stay private, which you definitely don't wanna be on except if you're not it means no one has noticed that you even exist.

Tom   So ... the funny or maybe sad thing about Bartok's third piano concerto is that he died before he finished it. He was writing it for his wife's birthday; he was gonna surprise her and I guess he did—but not in the way he was going for.

And the funny or maybe sad thing about that afternoon when I was playing it is that Mr. Damion, the chair of the music department at Carpenter, this total walking prick—I mean, the guy literally looks like a penis—well, he walked right into the room, and there I am, on top of the tiny percussion teacher, playing her like a fucking symphony.

And ... um.

The least funny thing about what happens next is that she says I came onto her. And also, that I was aggressive or something.

Amber   At some point later it occurs to you that maybe sex should actually be a *pleasant* experience. But how to make that happen is a whole other thing. I mean, how can you control what kind of sex you're about to have? You usually don't know until you're in it. Or maybe not even til after it's over. Like days or weeks or even *years* in the past. Which is what I try to tell Heather, but she's very definite about things, so she's just like: if he raped you, he raped you, okay? And I'm like "okay!!"

Tom   I mean, credit to my mom, because she didn't believe it for a second ... Said it was racism. Plain and simple. And, you know ... maybe it was.

Maybe it was.

Ms. Mackey got fired, so I guess that's ... But then everyone asks why she's gone so by December of my junior year, I'm the guy who fucked this sweet little teacher literally and figuratively, even though we didn't actually fuck, and I have to see this shrink because what if I'm like totally depraved, which seemed like such a joke.

Amber *and* **Tom**   But now

Amber   I realize it's my default state. This zone of wanting something and not wanting it at the same time. And, like, what happened with Zach was a big example of that.

Tom   Leslie looks at me and says "this is about you and Amber Cohen. I believe you two are acquainted." And then there's this silence while my brain computes that. Me and Amber Cohen. And my first thought is she did something weird, like maybe she's in trouble for doing something really fucking weird, but then I look at his face and I can tell it's not that.

Amber   Zach's my friend Rachel's brother, this totally white bread frat guy type, not the brightest bulb but *cute*, you know? And I liked him probably in large part because he never seemed to know who I was, even though I was over at Rachel's all the time and always tried to look nice for him but also not like I was *trying* to look nice because you can't seem to be trying to look nice when you're going over to your friend's house to do Latin homework.

Tom   And he starts talking about "Title IX" and how it's his responsibility to oversee all investigations of conduct that might have violated the policy. And he's speaking really carefully and not making eye contact and it's making me feel like I did when I was going out with this girl Alexa at Carpenter who was actually a sort of minor celebrity—like she had this blog that I never read but white people like Lena Dunham were all excited about it or something? I didn't care; she was hot and we'd go to her apartment after school and no one was ever home and then one afternoon I was sitting around in my *underwear* and her mother just, like, walks in and Alexa is all, "oh this is Tom; I told you about Tom, didn't I?" which she clearly hadn't, and the mother acts as though she's so excited to see me there, which she clearly isn't, and the whole thing is so uncomfortable and I sort of knew that if I'd been a different guy she would have sent me home on the spot but instead there I was having *dinner* with them and being talked to like *I* was the celebrity, like they'd be so disappointed when I'd finally have to leave.

Amber   I was a senior in high school and I'd just gotten into college. Like, *that day*, I mean.

I'd come home from school and I was scrolling through this really dumb email where you have to rank like the five best books you've ever read and then send it onto the second person on the list and I was trying to decide whether to make my number one, like, *Gone Girl* or *The Iliad*, when I see I have a new email and the subject line is "Welcome to … " but you can't see the whole thing, so I open it and it's Princeton.

Tom   I'm like what policy, Leslie? I honestly don't know what he's … But then he says "sexual misconduct." … And he says it strangely loud, like he's embarrassed, which embarrasses *me*. See, I've never had any clue what to do with someone who's trying to hide how they feel … probably because *I* am always trying to hide how I feel.

Amber   Which is … I mean, I was NOT expecting to get in. I really wasn't, even though being a mediocre squash player can help a lot because colleges need to fill their teams, and there just aren't enough really excellent squash players. But still I didn't expect anything that good to happen to me. I was always kind of not the best at anything, you know?

Like, I was never the *prettiest* girl. Not, like, ugly. I mean, I *can* actually look in the mirror and see a person who's kind of attractive, looking back at me. I don't know. My mom told me once I was "pretty enough" which one hundred percent of shrinks would probably agree explains everything.

Tom   So I'm just like … what?? And he says it even louder, even though the problem wasn't that I didn't hear him.

Amber   The day I got into Princeton was the second night of Passover and Rachel had invited me to her family's seder. But I mean, who does the *whole* service on the SECOND night? And not only that but her dad asks everyone at the seder to discuss things, like why is it worse to be indifferent than stupid? In reference to the four sons. And why do we say next year in Jerusalem?

And before I know what I'm doing I'm looking right at Zach and saying something about Jews and longing, and I know my face is very very red and kind of splotchy. Which is what happens when I'm embarrassed, so the whole world can see exactly how I'm feeling at all times.

Tom   So, just to be clear … Amber says I violated the policy? And he says yes, she has lodged a complaint. And I'm like "but that girl is seriously into me" and he gives me this look like I'm deluded. (*A realization.*) Which I guess I am.

Amber   After the seder, we're all just hanging out, and Zach wants to watch hockey because the Rangers are having an okay season so they're "worth watching", but, you know, they lose. In like overtime.

And Zach is not happy. I guess he's one of those beleaguered fans who takes everything really hard, and he's like "I'm gonna have a fucking drink" which makes it sound like he hadn't *already* been drinking all night long, but now he switches to beer, even though it has barley or wheat in it or whatever and isn't something you're supposed to have during Passover. But he's just like "fuck it. The Rangers weren't supposed to lose during Passover either." Which doesn't make any sense.

Tom   I ask him: what exactly does she say I did? And what you can see of Leslie behind that beard turns this bright shade of red and he's like "she says you raped her, Thomas" … and I can't help it but I start to cry.

Amber   Rachel had fallen asleep on the couch, and Zach asked if I wanted to see this app on his phone that's like an updated version of *Angry Birds Star Wars*, but really he just wanted me to come sit next to him because once I was there he kind of touched my wrist and I froze and of course he knew. I mean, really he'd probably known

Amber *and* **Tom**   For years

Tom   my dad was a star. A math wiz, a point guard, a model son. But by the end of high school he was drinking, and getting into fights, and he never made it to college, which haunted him forever. And here *I* am, at *Princeton,* sitting across from Leslie, who asks what questions I have about the rape I may or may not have committed within the first two months of school. And then there they are too, creeping into the corners of your mind: those men swaying in the trees, because they're always there.

Amber   And he stands and kind of pulls me up with him, and we go to his room and he's kinda stumbly drunk and I am completely sober and we fall onto the bed and he is not exactly gentle with me but I don't really mind; the next day I get a UTI and it hurts so bad, but I don't know that right now and eventually he takes his fingers out of me and squeezes one of my boobs really hard, and I moan a little because I think that's what people do but he puts his finger to his mouth like I've made this faux pas by making a sound, a gesture I remember at least subconsciously because now I am always silent during sex, always always, like you practically don't know I'm there, and then he climbs on top of me and sticks it in. And the whole time, which isn't a long time, I keep thinking "I got into college today" which, in conjunction with what's happening right now, makes me feel like a … yeah, like a different person, I guess. And when he's done he grunts a little, like this sound is just getting pushed out of him and it's not exactly a happy

sound, but still I feel weirdly privileged—and in all honesty, grown up—
to know what Zach Lieberman sounds like when he comes.

Tom   And I just blurt out: I'm innocent until proven guilty, right? And
Leslie looks kind of apologetic and then, really gently, is like: yes and
no … In the coming weeks, before the hearing, there will absolutely be
a comprehensive investigation … but also you should know that college
campuses are not the criminal justice system. There's no judge or jury.
A panel of three "neutral" appointees will interview you and Amber and
any witnesses to try to get a full picture of what happened and then we
will "convene" altogether and discuss. And I'm like "thanks, Leslie"
and he's like "of course, Tom" so, like, I guess he thought I was being
sincere.

Amber   It snowballed. I'm suddenly the most interesting person
Heather has ever met and she wants to be with me all the time. She
even waits in the hall when I go talk to this guy Leslie, whom I'd
just assumed was going to be a woman because of the name and also
because here was someone whose job was to talk to predominantly
female *rape victims*.

Amber   But it wasn't.

Tom   But I wasn't.

Tom   And Leslie says if the panel determines that a preponderance of
the evidence suggests I did it, he will be brought in to help determine my
penalty. And I'm like "what??" and he says: if they find that the claim is
more likely true than not true," which is still sounding kinda opaque to
me, and he's like, "fifty percent plus a feather, that's what it's like", and
I picture this two sided scale, and each side has the same amount on it,
the very same shit, but wait, what's that up there? Oh, it's a feather, and
it comes drifting down from the sky … and lands on one side of the scale
and suddenly that side is weighted down beyond belief. Suddenly there's
no contest.

Amber   I tell Leslie that *Bob,* my stepdad, says I have to be really
careful about accusing a Black man of … And the way Leslie looks at
me, even though he doesn't say anything, makes me worry that Tom
isn't gonna get a fair trial, like he's gonna be one of those Black men just
tossed recklessly into the tornado of a broken system, but then I realize
that shouldn't really matter to me. I can't fix the system, can I?

Tom   So the panel of three neutral appointees is made up of a white
dude who's like the assistant *assistant* dean of students, this hippy-ish art

professor who looks white to me but her last name is Diaz; and a Black woman in the *women's studies* department. Which is like, really?

Amber   And then Leslie is like: "but are you sure you clearly expressed your "lack of affirmative consent"? This is, after all, a very serious accusation, young lady" and he's staring at me hard, like it would suit him just fine if I walked right on out of his office and his life, and for the first time I flash back to the night in question and to the way I felt the next morning, how I wanted to get out of Tom's room as quickly as humanly possible, and dig a hole and just live there forever, and I'm like "I'm sure, Leslie, but thank you for reiterating the gravity of my actions."

Tom   He puts his hand on my shoulder and is like "call me if you need anything" and I have the sensation I always have when someone tries to be paternal, which is pretty much uncontrollable rage mixed with deep-seated resentment and I brush his hand off my shoulder as though it was a bug and he flinches like I hit him or something.

Amber   Linda is also there with me, at the trial. She's my lawyer. That creeper Leslie told me I could bring one person with me to any discussion related to the investigation—a friend, a relative, an advisor or a lawyer. So duh I go with a lawyer.

Tom   I am all alone. I don't even tell my mother about this. It reminds me of this time in 9th grade when my mom came to see me in the school play and she got all dressed up and was so proud but the thing is—I never stepped foot on that stage. I was in the third floor computer room making out with this girl Julia, who was also in the chorus and when we realized we missed the beginning we didn't know what to do so we just stayed there and later my mom was like "you were just so good in that play." And I never told her it wasn't true.

Amber   Bob found Linda for me. He's a lawyer too and needs to feel important so he's always like "lemme help you with that." Bob is this tiny man and so maybe he has to compensate. I don't know what my mom was thinking. It might seem weird to say so, but my dad was a very attractive man. Even when he was frail. Like I once overheard my mom on the phone snorting and saying "well, at least he's still virile." Which is not really the way you want to think about your dad. Or maybe it is?

Tom   I think I went to a debate in the first week of school in this room. It was on whether or not Guantanamo Bay was constitutional, and this one dude was so crazy passionate about it being unconstitutional that I started to agree with the other side, just because they weren't so annoying, and the whole time then and the whole time now I'm like how do you defend yourself? Is it what you say or how you say it?

Amber   So when we're all there—

Tom   The chair of the panel stands up and says "Welcome, all." As though we're at a church service or something.

Amber *and* **Tom**   "Welcome."

Tom   We're here today to decide whether or not Thomas Anthony committed a violation of the sexual misconduct policy on October 23rd in connection with his interactions with his fellow student—

Amber *and* **Tom**   "Amber Cohen."

Amber   And when they say my name it's like, whoa. This is really happening.

Tom   Then I guess we're each supposed to make a statement. I am made aware of this because the panel chair is like "Tom. Amber. Now you will each make a statement."

Amber   Here's a statement for you: the beginning of college was INSANE. I can barely remember it; that's how insane it was.

I drank a lot. Like, a lot a lot. And it tastes so foul but you just keep drinking it.

It's not peer pressure so much as fear. Like, if I don't do this, I might have to think about who I am and where I am and all of that is just too …

It was nice to be on the squash team, because you have this kind of … this built-in group of friends. Or at least people who could be your friends if you liked them. I mean, you see them all the time. The thing about doing a sport in college is that you do it all the time.

And, like, Heather was on the team too and she lived on my hall, so it actually would have been like weird and conspicuous if we *weren't* friends.

And Heather came from a lot of money. You could just tell. And that's not a knock on her at all, it was just … you could tell.

And she had a boyfriend from home, Dave, who was at Georgetown now, and she was always getting What'sApp messages from him and laughing hysterically. I guess Dave was really funny or something.

I don't know. Heather and I spend a lot of time together, and she shows me how I've been plucking my eyebrows all wrong and she shows me how to drink demurely from a flask. Also she buys me a flask.

We go out every night because everyone goes out every night. And then you go to classes and then you read—and there is so much to read; every day you have like hundreds of pages assigned but you only have between let's say four and seven to do all that reading because after seven you have to go out and drink till you're sick but those afternoon hours are exactly when, if you're on a team, you're at practice. So there's no time to do any of that reading and it starts to build up and even by the end of the first week there's this voluminous amount of reading you haven't done and this equally voluminous terror and *that's* what keeps you drinking.

Tom   Amber makes a really brief statement about how regrettable this whole thing is and how she wishes it hadn't come to this. And I'm like, you know, if you wished that you had it in your power to make it happen.

Amber   And then Tom makes his statement. He's like a) we were drunk and b) I would never rape someone. He can't even say "rape"—he takes this enormous pause before he says it like there's something in his mouth that's causing him great pain but which would be even more painful if it managed to escape.

Tom   I don't want to be here. It's all that goes through my head. I don't want to be here.

Amber   I don't like that Tom is all alone. He's like all alone at this long table.

Tom   I start thinking about when I first got to school, and how … yeah, how nervous I was. I mean, nobody brought me to college. My Mom didn't, like, come with me and unpack my clothes and make my bed for me. Nobody took me to the store to buy that sticky-stuff you use to put up posters, that doesn't leave a mark on the walls. Nope, I took the bus and then dragged myself and two crappy suitcases across campus.

And then halfway across the quad, one of those shitty suitcases just cracks wide open so there I am gathering as much of my stuff as I can in my arms and trying to look like it doesn't matter one bit. Finally this guy who's like the Indian Channing Tatum or something comes over and is like "need a hand?" and that was Sunil. He went and got me some garbage bags and we shoved everything into them so I show up to my room hauling what looks like this gigantic load of trash, but, you know, it's how I met the best friend I ever had, so I guess, in a way, I'm grateful.

Not that Sunil and me were tight from the start. I didn't see him again for a week, and it was possibly the weirdest week in my life, when you're sort of trying to fit in but you're not sure yet you even want to. I mean, seriously—part of you just wants to put all your stuff in your one remaining suitcase and go back the way you came. It's overwhelming—people are *all over you* to join their newspaper or their Motown-only a capella group, or the Black Student Union and you feel sort of sorry for them and also guilty for not wanting any of it. I mean, *you're* just like trying to figure out where the damn bathrooms are. And how to get from your room to where you can *eat* things.

And yeah, maybe you kinda miss home. Or not like, home, but the idea of it.

Like, maybe you start to realize you've moved on from something. And you're never going back.

Amber   Linda, my lawyer, told me not to mention enjoying myself for some of the night. So I didn't say anything about my emotional state. About how just looking at Tom makes me tingly all over, so much so that sometimes I need to go home and change my underwear, which is gross but also a totally natural phenomenon as any high school health teacher would have you know. I didn't say that every night I imagined Tom slipping into my dorm room, unannounced, crawling into my bed and just having me.

Tom   Oh, and thank you Princeton. I almost forgot. They gave me a black roommate. Wasn't that thoughtful? Only Jayson was from San Francisco and into, like, fashion and didn't know a thing about music. He was always telling me how I could "dress for success", which apparently meant never wearing any of the clothes I actually owned, and of course I assumed he was gay so on one of the first nights I'm like "so what's it like being gay?" and he gives me this weird look. Whatever. I'm sure he figured it out sooner or later.

So at the end of that first week the only thing I wanted was to find a piano and be alone. I'm hung-over from all the Jell-o shots; I can't get the taste of keg beer outta my mouth; I can't find my jacket which I musta left somewhere. So I'm cold and I have this headache and so far the food—it's like there is just never enough food to fill me up, or I feel like I have to leave the dining hall because I have a sense that I need to do something but almost immediately after I've left I realize I'm starving.

I'm just feeling depleted, you know? And my mom sounds a little tired on the phone, like not as interested in what's going on with me as I would expect. But whatever. If I find a piano, I'll be okay.

So I'm wandering like a jackass up and down Nassau Street looking for Woolworth, the music department, which isn't even on that street but me and maps, we do not get along—when I hear my name. And it's Sunil. And he's leaning against a wall under this stone arch and he's like "you have to hear this" and he shoves his iPhone at me and I kid you not the guy is listening to Mozart's Piano Concerto No. 9, which is one of my all-time all-time favorites. And he's like "isn't that *astonishing*?" And it was.

Amber   And then they start asking questions. And the questions are almost as embarrassing as the answers.

Tom   The white dude is like: you're saying it was consensual? And I'm like, yeah … what I can remember was consensual. That's right.

Amber   And then the art professor asks how much I had to drink and when I drank and how much time elapsed between drinks.

And I wanna be like—that's the point of drinking! So you don't remember how many drinks you've had and how much time has elapsed between drinks. But I know I can't say that.

Tom   Some of the questions we wrote ahead of time to ask each other.

Amber   I think this must be one of Tom's questions: Amber, did you feel you had something to prove that night? And I'm like "no." And Linda puts her hand on my knee, which is her way of saying "no need to elaborate." But when I think about it, I guess I think that when I got to school I should've said I had a boyfriend at home because *Heather* got to be this outside observer, staring down at us all. And by night ten or twelve the pressure is huge and Heather was always next to me going "what about him?" and invariably pointing to some loser and I'd be like "*that's* what you think of me?" but end up hooking up with him anyway just to get her off my back.

Tom   They ask whether anything else was going on with me that might have contributed to my behavior that night. And because Amber isn't really answering the questions, I'm just like, "nope." Nothing else going on with me.

Amber   I look at him, and I'm like "really Tom?" Because it really really seemed like something was going on with him. That night.

Tom   Sunil is like my spirit guide, my maestro, my first base coach, my brother. I follow him around like a fuckin' cat in heat. I just have this *reverence* for the guy.

He's from Florida, some town where he was the only person under, like, ninety-five for miles around, and his family owns a few restaurants now but for so many years they were just poor, just like dirt poor. His dad couldn't get work and at one point his mom and one of his sisters moved back to India. They went back to *India* because shit was gonna be better *there*. So Sunil was left with his dad. They literally started with a cart. One of those food carts and the two of them cooked everything and it took years but then it caught on.

He said the violin saved him. He played it all his life. And to hear him play is a fucking miracle. That's how good he is.

You know how some people love a book and they read it again and sorta get new things out of it? That never really happened to me. But with music. With music, it happens all the time. And Sunil. He wasn't anything like me but he got that and so he was completely like me.

And it occurred to me how lucky it was that I didn't realize, growing up, you know, like, how alone I'd been.

I tried to explain it, on the phone, to my mom, and she was just like "Tommy, you had friends. You've always had friends" so yeah, she didn't get it.

And you know, she was just sounding so tired.

But then I thought it was just that I was so fatigued myself because I wasn't sleeping because, you know, every night it was one of these parties, or three of them. And every night I was having sex.

Amber   I notice him for the first time in Intro Psych. He's sitting off to my left, a couple rows ahead of me, and his head is jerking forward every few minutes in that way that happens when you can't stay awake. He's making a really valiant effort though and at one point I see him literally hold his eyes open with his fingers and he is also constantly shifting in his chair. So all of that catches my attention, and also, and this probably sounds, like … but yeah, that he's Black. I notice that too.

Tom   At some point Sunil is like "man, you should slow it down." And I'm like "why?" And he points out—because *he's* a nice guy—that a couple times, these girls have sent these crazy transparent messages like "hey, did I maybe leave a lip gloss in your room?" or "I wasn't gonna get in touch but I had this weird dream last night and you were in it!" but I'm like screw that. I'm a freshman. It's the first month of school.

And instead I start to get on him about why he's *not* hooking up. Because these girls are just there for the picking and every night he hangs back. I'm like "dude, what're you doing??" and one night he says he's not feeling well and another night he has a leg cramp and another night he doesn't see anyone "remotely interesting." And I'm like "interesting? These girls don't gotta be interesting." And I can tell there's some part of him that thinks I'm a dick and also some part of him that likes that about me. But he doesn't give in. He's just like "Tommy-boy, you do your thing. I'm heading home." And after five nights of that, I pounce. I'm drunk off my ass and I get in his face, like "yo, what the fuck are you doing? This isn't gonna happen every day for the rest of your life, you know" and by this point we've walked out onto the quad and I'm so wasted that I'm seeing stars or maybe there really are that many stars over New Jersey, and I am so pissed at him and love him like a brother— maybe even more than my actual brothers—that I am shaking him a little, like shaking his shoulders and feeling really righteous and like I'm helping a brother out and teaching him what's right while at the same time justifying all the choices that *I've* ever made, that when he kisses me I am more shocked and repulsed and freaked out than I've ever been in my entire life.

Amber   But, like, I'm a big fan of Black people. I don't want to be so naïve as to say Jews and African-Americans have all this stuff in common, but they have some stuff in common, like not really wanting to go camping, or to Nantucket, and also the deep and unwavering fear that at any moment they will be rounded up and killed.

And like, I just, I notice him. That's all.

Tom   The weird thing is that after Sunil like *assaults* me with his tongue, we're actually okay.

We don't even talk about it.

I mean, it was clear that I didn't want anything to do with any of that, but he didn't seem hurt or anything. Which is actually kind of amazing, right? And I start to have a little insight. Like maybe this is why guys do that. Something doesn't work out, you just move on. Not like every single female I have ever known who is physically incapable of moving on even if you make out once for five minutes on a fucking dance floor.

Amber   After I notice him in Intro Psych, I start seeing him everywhere. I turn around and he's a few people behind me in line in the dining hall with like five waffles on his tray; he's walking across the quad with this ripped Indian guy, who looks kinda like Channing Tatum if he was Indian, like he's really bulked up, which you don't expect with Indian guys no offense.

Tom   And then one day at the end of Intro Psych, Sunil's like "dude, you *are* aware of the fact that this girl can't stop staring at you" and I'm like "who?" and he points to someone a couple rows behind me and she's really hot, like kind of a Chrissy Teigen / Kate Upton type, skinny but with enormous tits, and I'm like "wow" and he's like "no, the one next to her" and the one next to her is not as good, but you know, I'm equal opportunity.

Amber   I see him sleeping in Firestone, the library, and I see him in the doorway of PJ's Pancake House, and I see him at the gym where he's maybe technically lifting weights but mostly just talking to that Indian guy. One night I see him making out with this tiny Korean girl at T.I. and he's so into it it's like he's *eating* her face, and normally I would think that was gross but for some reason this time I *don't*.

Tom   So I go and talk to her. Why not, right?

Amber   He comes up to me after Psych and is just like, "hey."

Tom   And she's like, "hey."

Amber   And it occurs to me that maybe he's been seeing me everywhere too!

A new disappointing discovery.

And maybe he thinks I've been stalking him??

And then I get self-conscious. And *then* I think that maybe actually he's talking to Heather, and I just hugely embarrassed myself, but no ... it really does seem like he's talking to me.

Tom   For some reason, I lose my smooth. Like, I don't know what to say next. And we kinda stare at each other until finally I'm like:

So how's psych treating you?"

Amber   Oh! It's okay.

Tom   Yeah?

Amber   Yeah.

Tom   Cool.

Amber   Yeah.

Beat.

Tom   So, so far we're having a really interesting conversation.

Sunil's right behind me and kinda jumps in. He makes a bad joke, at least I think it's a joke? about how we're probably missing out on some critical exploration of the human condition by always falling asleep in this lecture so maybe she could help fill us in, and I'm thinking, holy shit, Sunil is NOT good at talking to the ladies. And then this girl, this— sorry—kinda mousy girl who looks like she could be any of the girls at Carpenter whose Bat Mitzvahs I went to every weekend of 8th grade — this girl turns to me and is like "I'm afraid you might have gotten the impression that I've been following you or something"—which by the way I hadn't, *at all*—"but I really have just been struck by how we seem to move along the same paths or in the same circles or something, like I saw you in the gym and at PJ's and weren't you at the Bent Spoon too—the ice cream place? And isn't it crazy" and all that and I'm just, like, who is this girl??

Then her friend, the hot one, is like "Amber, I think he just wants your notes" and poor Amber turns beet fucking red and you can see her mind just unraveling. She's like:

Amber *and* **Tom**   "Oh, right, duh."

Tom   And then these kinda splotchy spots start to appear all over her neck and before I can even help it I'm like "nah, I wasn't after yer notes. I saw you that time, at the Bent Spoon, right?" even though I haven't once gotten ice cream since I got here and would never pay five dollars for a tiny scoop of gourmet anything, but I don't know what's up with me; I keep going: "and I was thinking we could go back there together, like on purpose this time."

Amber   The funny thing or maybe it was just weird was that I'd never actually seen him at the ice cream place. As soon as I said it I knew it was wrong; I was just running at the mouth the way I do sometimes, and sometimes as a result not everything I say is one hundred percent wholly and completely true. I mean, maybe it's just that ice cream is never far from my mind. Or maybe I just wanted it to be true but either way we do end up getting ice cream the next day and he offers to buy mine, which even though I demur because I'm the product of feminists who worked really hard to have the right to buy their own ice cream, the offer means

we're on a real date, right? Me and 'Thomas Anthony,' who, I mean,
even his name is hot, and who knows, maybe he's gonna be my first real
boyfriend, not counting my camp boyfriend, which in all honesty was a
relationship based almost entirely on correspondence. Anyway I can't
really believe it, and I'm trying not to think about all the other things
I should be doing, like seriously the call of those books stacked on my
desk is deafening, and also I didn't work out as hard as I usually do this
afternoon, I don't know why, and now this ice cream that I can't help but
eat all of is gonna make me fat, I can feel myself getting fatter as I eat it,
not that I have eating issues, I mean, I don't, aside from the way all girls
have eating issues, which is that we think about what we eat 100 percent
of the time and always wanna kill ourselves.

Tom   Okay, so she's, like, weird.

I mean, she talks fast, like Usain Bolt-fast, and she doesn't really
look at me.

But she's not shy, exactly. I've been with shy girls before. This isn't
really shy. This is more like … yeah, weird, I guess.

Amber   But it doesn't matter. I'm on a date with this guy who for some
reason I noticed and it turned out he noticed me too, and *this* is why I'm
here, right? For experience, not just to read books I'll forget a month
after reading them, and life is short, I know it is; I've had that feeling
in my gut since I was a little kid, and it's not just because my dad was
older and was always maybe about to die, it's something that was in me,
was just *in* me, this sense that you can't hold onto anything and every
moment is over before it's even begun.

Tom   Not like there's something wrong with her. She's just *awkward*
and I'd like to say I find it cute or something, but really I just feel
awkward too, until she's like "god, I'm so awkward, aren't I" and
without meaning to I'm like "yeah, I guess" and she apologizes and
laughs in this way that *is* kinda cute and says she's gonna stop eating her
ice cream because she's SO full, and she puts it down, but a minute or
two later she picks it up and finishes it anyway.

And then she's like:

Amber   So what's up with your friend?

Tom   What?

Amber   That hot Indian guy.

Tom   You mean Sunil?

Amber   How many hot Indian guys do you hang around with?

Tom   And for a second I'm sorta taken aback, like despite myself, because does she think Sunil is hotter than me?

But then she adds:

Amber *and* **Tom**   Not that he's hotter than you, Thomas Anthony.

Tom   I mean, she is already calling me *Thomas Anthony*! Which is something only my mom has called me, and only when she's mad or like being really lovey with me, but this weird girl starts it up right away, which is what I mean when I said she wasn't really shy; I mean, she's actually kinda straight up confident except that she can't look me in the eye and she can't stop talking.

Amber   A little thing about Judaism? When something good happens to you, you just assume something bad is on the way. That's the way Jews exist in the world, and also we have a very hard time walking around knowing about all the bad things happening at every moment in every part of the world, like if you watch that Naomi Watts movie about the tidal wave in 2004, then afterwards you're gonna Google the *shit* out of it and find this account of a guy who stayed up in a *tree* while everyone he knew got swept away, at which point you can't stop thinking about the last moments those people had alive and their fear, and also the pain they left in their wake. When this kid I didn't know well, but had known since preschool, so I *knew* him, you know? … when he killed himself in 11th grade, it occurred to me just how deafening and enormous the grief must be that emanates off the surface of this earth. Like, our atmosphere must just be filled with all this airless sorrow.

Tom   "Is he a nerd in a not nerd's body?" She's *still* talking about Sunil, and I really don't wanna be thinking about his body right now, I mean cool it, girl, who just took you for ice cream?, so I'm like "nah, he's chill" and she's like "okay but, like, didn't I notice he had a violin case" and so then I have to get into the whole music thing and she's all "wow. WOW, you two sound like professional musicians. So is that why you came to Princeton? To pursue music?" And she's looking at me in this way that I can't explain and before I know it I'm saying "I can't think about music like it's work because I need *something* in my life that's an escape from everything else." I mean, I tell this girl that I need to *escape*. And she nods like she understands, and then says:

"So why did you come here?" Which to me is, like, obvious: because I aced my SATs, and I got in; you don't *not* go to Princeton, and she's like "I was attracted to the university's very strong English and creative writing department. See, my only minor talent is in writing so I have to pursue that path because really I think we pursue what we feel we're decent at because why set ourselves up for total abject failure." That's what Amber Cohen is like.

Amber *and* **Tom**   I'm telling you.

Amber   Like after that kid died, and his name was Jonathan, I feel like I should say his name, I was Skyping with Rachel about how horrible it was, how we just felt empty and like we had no business being alive, when one of my camp friends messaged me too, wondering if I could send her a photo of me from 9th grade because she was about to get that same haircut and wanted to show her stylist, so I'm having these two simultaneous conversations, one about the utter existential pain of living and the other about whether that was my haircut in 9th grade or maybe she means the one during the 10th grade chorus trip to Budapest—and really that just about sums up life, doesn't it?

A new idea, definitive.

Only it doesn't. Because it leaves out so much. Like when my dad died, I was just numb for so long. For so long I walked through my life without really living it, just years of school, squash, homework, in this endless cycle, and feeling like if I had something great to say there wouldn't be anyone there to hear it because my dad was many things—a product of his time and of growing up Jewish in the South, which probably made him irascible and insecure but he would always listen to me and seemed to care what I had to say and when he was gone … that was gone too. And somewhere deep inside, I think I felt like I was due for something good to happen, and when I got into Princeton it seemed like maybe that was my dad's doing, like a balancing of the scales.

Tom   Never in the past, not once, yo, have I gotten such a hard time for *not* making a move on a date. I mean, I went with her for fucking ice cream, for godsake.

Amber   But Thomas Anthony felt like too much. I mean not only was he by far the hottest person who had ever noticed me, but behind that layer of swagger and charm, he was also frankly the nicest. All of which is to say: he didn't kiss me that night. And I couldn't tell what that meant. I mean, maybe it was because all we'd done was get ice cream like fifth graders so afterwards it made sense to go our separate ways.

Or … maybe it was … me.

Something to do with me.

Tom   An *hour* later, I get this message on Facebook:

"Dear Tom."

Amber (*bashful*)

I couldn't help myself.

Tom   "Just to be clear, I really enjoyed hanging out with you. I wasn't sure, based on the way our date (was it even a date?) ended—the way you said "okay, so see ya around" that you would wanna see me again but I wanted to let you know that I'd be more than game to give it another go because I feel like I still have so much to teach you about the world, Thomas Anthony, like the proper way to eat an ice cream cone (which is not all in one bite) and how to pronounce your linguistics teacher's name. (I spent a summer in Wales.) And if that doesn't tempt you completely, I don't know what will. ☺

Amber   I was really torn about the use of an emoticon, which any self-respecting person should be, but then again I was torn about sending the message at all, so I figured what the hell.

Also the hour I spent writing that message was more time than I'd spent focused on any single thing up to that point in my college career.

Tom   I don't know if I'd been planning to go out with her again. Probably not, if I'm being honest. Some guys get off on a girl being aggressive but for me it's the other way around. If I'm being honest. Like, you know, let ME make the moves.

But in the case of Amber, I remembered this thing she'd said when we were ordering our ice cream, like "isn't it funny how incapacitating having choices is" or something like that, and also she isn't quite as, like, mousy as I first thought, like actually her eyes are sorta weird and sad and pretty when she actually looks at you, and the one time she actually looked at me, when I was saying goodbye, I was so taken aback that I just took off.

So I wrote her back. I mean, I waited a week, but I wrote her back.

Amber   He waited *a week*. And, like, I saw him around and had to pretend I hadn't written that stupid thing.

Tom   Sunil was like, "dude, you're blowing her off" and he seemed really amused by the whole thing, and strangely, like, interested in Amber. Like in what I knew about her, and I was like "I don't know, dude, she's just sort of a weirdo" and he's like "but you like her" and I'm like "I don't know." And he seems really suspicious about why I haven't had a real relationship before and I'm like dude I'm eighteen; I don't need to settle down. And he's like "but I bet your Mom would like if you did" and I don't know how he knows that, but my Mom *is* always like "Thomas, you could make some young lady so happy, why do you insist on torturing these women?" But I can't admit that so I'm just like, "get off my back" and then he says, really simply, "what are you looking for, man? What do you think you're gonna find?" And I almost tell him the truth, which is that I have this sort of 3am fear, this desperate like night of the soul fear, that I will never really find my way around this world and that whatever I do I won't amount to anything …

And this might be why I write Amber back. Because she looked at me as though I really might pursue something.

Amber   He Snapchats me: "Amber, wanna meet at Cap tonight? Kegger."

And I can't help it. I write back

Amber *and* **Tom**   Right away

Tom   I get a message back. Like, within two minutes.

This girl has no fucking game, right?

But that's okay, I guess. I mean, so she has no game. So what.

Amber   I don't know what to wear so I just go with a sort of tried and true look—the tank under a blazer with tight jeans and tall boots look. And I used the more expensive of my two shampoos and I even read two pages of my psych textbook before going out and they happened to be about the pratfall effect which explains why people actually are *attracted* to people who aren't perfect, who are clumsy or flawed in some way, and I found that really encouraging and the timing, like, really fateful.

And that afternoon I'd spoken to my Mom, which is hit or miss because sometimes she only talks about herself, which is my fault for asking her so many questions but I always want to see if she'll realize she hasn't asked me anything and turn it towards me of her own accord. But this time I think there was some undeniable quality in me—happiness, I guess—and she could just tell and she was like "Amber?" and I said, "you know, I think I'm gonna like it here" which is obviously a quote from *Annie*, a movie I watched about a zillion times when I was a kid, so much so that I think the movie and my childhood are sort of synonymous. Which made her cry a little. To think of me happy. Because that's just not always true. Of me.

Tom   Right before I'm supposed to meet up with Amber, I'm pre-gaming with Sunil. We're three shots of Jagermeister and a couple Sam Adams in when my phone rings and it's my mom—and she's just like "Tommy, I've got it." The big fucking C. Cancer. She says she doesn't want me to give it a single thought and she's fine; it's not such a bad kind of cancer and I should enjoy college and I'm like you know I can't do that and she starts to cry and she says "Tommy, what'll kill me quicker than cancer is if you don't take every advantage of your time at school" and what can I say to that? My brothers didn't go to college, my dad—nope—and the closest my mom came was three months of nursing school. So she's wailing and I'm all "okay, okay, of course I'll enjoy college" so I'm trying and Sunil and I go back to pre-gaming and talking and I'm already kinda drunk and it comes out, what she just told me, and Sunil—he just flat out bursts into tears. I mean, *I'm* not even crying but he cries for me and for my mom, who he's never even met and that moves me—that fuckin' moves me—and our man Mozart is playing in the background, Piano Concerto number 9, and Sunil puts his arms around me and I start to let it out; I let it out because I can't lose my mom; I can't lose my mom; she's been the glue binding me to this earth, I know it even if I've never said it out loud … and it's good to be held, it's nice to be held by my friend, to be in his arms; I even have this passing thought about how nice it must be to be Sunil's violin, this is how gentle he is, and even when he, like, rubs my back, that's okay; he's just there for me; he's just feeling it, but yeah …

When he tries to kiss me again … I mean, that's too much, that's a line crossed, that's me being taken advantage of right there and so I say so; I jump back and I say so, and he's like "Tommy. Come on, Tommy. You know you're in love with me. It's okay. We're in love."

Amber   Heather walked me to Cap even though I told her not to, and when we get there I'm waiting for her to leave. I just don't want to be with her when Tom arrives. Like I don't need a) the comparison and b) the suggestion that I didn't want to meet him on my own. I didn't want to seem nervous. Precisely because I was so nervous.

But Heather isn't getting the picture. So finally I have to just be like, "so maybe you should go now?" at which point she gets really huffy and is like "suit yourself" and as she walks off adds "nothing's gonna happen tonight anyway" which, like, infuriates me, because how does she know that? And so I call after her "who died and made you Humbert

Humbert?" and then to clarify, "an omniscient narrator" and she looks
back at me like "what??" and walks away.

Tom   And then there's this long pause and finally I'm like nope. Nope
you've got that wrong. I say you don't know the first thing about me and
you never will. I say you're an asshole and a fag and my mom has cancer
and what the fuck were you thinking? And I can't help it but I pick up
his violin and I smash it; I smash it into the ground and pieces of it fly
everywhere and Sunil screams as though I've hit him, or worse, and my
mother is sick and my friend, my only friend, is not my friend anymore
and I wanna puke it all up and get it out of my body, just out, just gone,
all of it, and then cleaned up and away, I want someone else to please
clean it up—please.

Amber   I was standing in the quad, waiting, taking little ladylike sips
from my flask and watching this kid—like he was definitely too young
to be a freshman—walk along the fence but he kept falling off it so it
wasn't really so impressive but still strangely compelling—to watch
someone keep failing at something—and I was like nota bene, Amber.
The pratfall effect at work again. How human it is to fail.

Tom   I don't know why but I kept thinking about Richard Wright's
Black Boy. We read it in 10th grade English. Like you know, even the
title. Even the title alone. I felt like everyone was looking at me because,
you know, they were. I mean, there were other kids from "under-served
communities" who got into Carpenter through this program Prep but my
year I was the only guy. And so most of my friends were white. And no.
I never told them that I felt at all … like, weird, going to their houses
after school and playing Xbox while their Black babysitters cooked and
cleaned and made us dinner.

And in English class we'd read aloud. And I remember having to read
this part of *Black Boy* that was like: "I live in this country where Black
people's aspirations are limited. So I had to go somewhere else to
do something to redeem my being alive." *To redeem my being alive.*
I remember that part. And I felt so much shame. And I felt so much
shame that I felt so much shame.

Amber   When Tom got there I could immediately tell he was in a
bad way. And in my head I was like "please don't end this. Don't say
you have to go home. Please." I tried to just keep him drinking so he
wouldn't leave. And, amazingly, that worked and eventually we went
inside and danced. He had his hand on my waist and he was kind of
holding on. Digging in. And I liked it. Feeling needed like that. But

I think I also knew that something wasn't right? And it made me so sad, that Tom might be sad. I mean what in the world should make Tom sad?

Tom   And suddenly she just takes her shirt off.

Amber   I mean, yeah I was drunk, but I'd been drunk before and never done that. I just had to do something to get rid of that look in his eyes.

Tom   I was like *what is going on*. Did we just walk into some alternate fucking universe where Amber Cohen takes her top off? ... But she looked happy. And free ... To this day, I'm not sure I've ever felt free like that.

Amber   We were in this crush of people. We were inside of it and moving with it and I loved it because I don't usually feel ... part of things in that way. And being there with Tom. That was like.

Tom   She looked ... yeah, she looked sexy, and I was like, let's get out of here.

Amber   And I took his hand and led him away. I felt like a character in someone else's story: Daisy and Gatsby, or that woman who worked at the department store in season one of *Mad Men* and Don Draper. I was just a girl pulling an attractive man out of a party with her.

Tom   Where do you wanna go?

Amber   Where do *you* wanna go?

Tom   I think I must've said we could go back to my place.

Amber   But first we just walked around. And made out. All over campus. It was ... amazing. I remember my hand in his, and the total thrill of wondering when we'd kiss next combined with the equal thrill of knowing it was going to happen. The *gift* of that.

Tom   When we got to my room, Jayson was there, sleeping; I must've thought he was sleeping. Or maybe I just wasn't thinking about Jayson.

Amber   He was sleeping. And we sort of tiptoe in, trying not to laugh. But there's this enormous poster on the wall, this Calvin Klein ad with Justin Bieber like naked, and I'm like what? And Tom is like "that is NOT mine I swear" and that cracks me up, and his roommate was like "shut the fuck up I'm trying to sleep" and then Tom was kissing me again.

Tom   I remember these little flashes of what came next ... Her back, this streak of white. And the light going on in the room, but I don't know who turned it on. I remember how good it felt to turn off my mind. The way you feel when you get lost inside a piece of music and the texture of it just envelops you and you're not in the world anymore; you're just part of the music.

Amber   I remember the weight of him on top of me and thinking he was different from Zach—not necessarily heavier, just different, like he was giving me more of himself, letting his weight just completely cover me up. I remember kissing him. I remember at some point really kissing him and thinking this guy was an excellent excellent kisser and worrying a little about that tuna sandwich I'd had at lunch while feeling simultaneously proud of myself for experiencing this unexpected thing, and very lucky.

Yeah. I think mostly I just felt really lucky.

Tom   The Latino one only uses the word coitus, not sex. Did Amber say anything, she asks, trying to sound neutral, when you were mid-coitus? Not that I remember, I tell them, always trying to smile as though I'm Mister fuckin' Rogers over here. How about "actually" the women's studies woman suggests. Did she say "actually" at any point?

Amber   There was this moment when suddenly it all just felt a little bit ... wrong.

Tom   No, I don't remember what she said or if she said anything but yeah, she probably didn't say yes. But, like, who says yes? Who in these situations is like "yes do that, please." We were drunk. She was into it ...

And if she wasn't into it at some point ... well then my body, my brain, convinced me she was. I wasn't knowingly ... I didn't do anything knowingly ... I know that.

Amber   Why would I have asked him to stop? You were into it at first. On this everyone agrees. And I really think about this. This zone of wanting something and not wanting it at the same time. Like I didn't ask Zach Lieberman to stop, and it's not like he was so gentlemanly. And now I am always silent during sex. I didn't ask Robby O'Neill in the 8th grade not to put his fingers inside of me on a dare in a closet, even though his thumbnail dug into me and it killed. I didn't say stop in 5th grade when Rachel and these two other girls were pulling my hair to see how long I could take it. I didn't say stop when my high school advisor suggested I take French and Latin and Ancient Greek *and* Japanese my junior year, even though when it comes down to it I much prefer English to any foreign language because how can you express yourself fully in a language that isn't your own? It's hard enough to express yourself in your own language. I didn't say stop when my mother told me not to eat carbohydrates if I ever wanted to get married. I didn't say stop when my dad died because I knew that was one thing I couldn't stop even if I tried, but still … I didn't even

Amber *and* **Tom**   Try

Tom   to remember what happened next they keep asking. And I am trying. But I can't get this moment out of my brain, this moment in the really early morning, when I woke up, and my face was tangled in her hair, like it was in my mouth and stuff. She was sleeping. Peacefully. And I saw the condom wrapper on the floor and was breathing a sigh of relief because I thought shit, Tom, you were so gone, something bad coulda happened. And then she opens her eyes and when she sees me she kinda startles a little, like she'd forgotten where she was. Then it's like she's about to say something but instead she just throws up all over the floor, just everywhere.

Amber *and* **Tom**   "I'm so sorry"

Tom   She keeps saying:

Amber *and* **Tom**   "I'm so sorry"

Tom   And I'm holding her hair back and I see just a little of the back of her neck and I swear I wanna, like, touch it, just a tiny bit with my thumb, which is weird because there she is puking but I feel something, like a longing for … Like maybe I do actually like this girl. After that she runs outta there pretty quick but I'm thinking she's embarrassed. And I clean it all up. It's fucking disgusting but I don't mind too much.

At some point, Jayson walks in like he's been up for hours already and run ten miles and designed a new messenger bag or some shit, and he's like, "good night?" in this snide little Jayson way and I don't say anything, and he's like "next time try not to fuck someone when I'm literally in the top bunk," and I'm like "I'm sorry, man," which I really was, and then, just to be sure, I say, "but she was into it, right?" And he gives me this look like "you're really gonna ask me that?" but still he said "well, she wasn't *not* into it, if that's what you're asking." And I *guess* that was what I was asking. And I was relieved.

Amber   At one point during the trial they start reading our text messages.

Tom   Like, *out loud*. And let me tell you it is really fucking weird to hear your own idiotic texts read out loud as, like … evidence.

Amber   *Hey Amber. I guess that was kind of weird. Ha. But I hope you're feeling better and you never vomit like that again in your life because that looked like deeply deeply unpleasant.*

I'm sorry I was in a sort of weird "frame of mind" yesterday. I hope I didn't freak you out or anything. I'm not really such an asshole. I promise. See you soon.—T.

And the even crazier thing is? I wrote back.

Tom   *Hey Tom. No worries. I mean yes it was a little weird but it's okay. I don't think you're an asshole.—A.*

So, like.

Amber *and* **Tom**   I don't know.

Tom   But I think: that's gotta score me some points. Her text back to me.

Amber   And then this awful professor—I've repressed her face she was that awful—I think she was in women's studies so she thinks she and I are … she thinks we are on, like, intimate terms. And she just asks the most graphic questions in the most matter-of-fact way, like "Amber, at what point did you feel Thomas Anthony's penis inside of you?"

Tom (*incredible to find yourself here*)   Thomas Anthony is what my mom calls me.

Amber   I mean, let's just be clear. We had sex. And I didn't say, like, "yes, fuck me. Do it in any way you want." So when they ask: "did this boy do this to you without your consent?" even though I might not have chosen that exact phrasing it seemed like the honest answer was yes, especially because I was probably too drunk to give any meaningful consent anyway—

Tom   You think *I* wasn't drunk?

Amber   And because Olivia, my RA, sat me down after Heather told her and I guess Olivia had been raped once too and she said "Amber you have to take this very seriously. If women don't take this very seriously it hurts all women. It affects all women."

Tom   Jayson comes into the hearing wearing this bow-tie like he's about to go have tea with the queen but what comes out of his mouth is

low-down and dirty; he says Amber couldn't have been conscious when
we were … He says he didn't hear a thing from her. But I'm like …
who would have a better sense of that? Me, or the guy on the top bunk?
I think there are things the body just *knows*, you know??

Amber   And then the assistant dean of students is like, "Amber, I want
you to pay very close attention to what I'm about to say" and he looks
around the room really intensely like a poor man's Gregory Peck giving
his closing statement in *To Kill a Mockingbird* and he says: "So everyone
agrees that earlier that night you took your shirt off. That you drank to
excess. That you very willingly went back to Tom's room and got into
his bed. Which makes me wonder: why do you think these actions that
you admit you freely took don't amount to some kind of tacit consent?"
And the panel is staring at me, one of the women looking kind of
annoyed with the tenor of the question, and the other one doing her best
to appear really neutral—which is when it occurs to me that maybe it
doesn't even matter what I say. Maybe these people will hear what they
want to hear no matter what. Maybe they decided in the first five minutes
what they thought happened, or even last week. And I'm processing that
and am just like "what?" and he says "you heard me" kind of harshly,
like a dare. And for the first time I really wanna leave the room, but
I can't, here I am, so I look down at my hands, and … I tell the truth.
Which is that I do remember it. This moment when all of a sudden he
was inside me, and it's not like I expected him to ask my permission
but I didn't expect him not to either. And it hurt and it kept hurting, and
eventually I just jumped out of bed.

Tom   Wait a second. No you didn't.

Amber   What?

Tom   You didn't jump out of bed.

Amber (*slowly*)   I thought you didn't remember.

Tom   I would remember that.

Amber   But you don't. You obviously don't because it happened.
I jumped out of bed and you grabbed me, hard, and I was like "actually,
um" but you pulled me back into bed and you just …

Tom   I didn't!

That's a lie—she didn't get out of bed; I know she didn't, and she
certainly didn't *jump* out of … Amber, tell them.

Amber   No I did. I had this strong physical impulse to get away from you, I did—

Tom   What are you talking about?

Amber   I'm just saying what happened—

Tom (*not able to help himself*)   You are such a privileged bitch, do you know that?

Amber   *I'm* privileged? I am? I know you want people to think you've had this awful life, but you haven't.

Tom   I want people to think that?

Amber   I bet you've always had friends. You've always had girls in love with you. You've always felt good about how you look. You get to be comfortable in your own body. And that's a privilege. *That's* a privilege.

Tom   It's a privilege to have everyone always looking at you? Is that right, Amber?

Amber (*really sincere*)   No one ever looks at me. So yeah. I think it is.

Tom   You're crazy if you think I'm comfortable in my own body.

Amber (*trying to figure it out*)   Well if you're not that might explain why you did this to me.

Tom   Why are *you* doing this to me? Because you think I've had it easy or something?

Amber   I don't think you've had it easy. I think you raped me.

Long beat.

Tom   And I hate her. In that moment I really fucking hate her. And I say so.

Amber (*suddenly quiet*)   You don't mean that … do you?

Tom   You're like this … flood of feelings that you just dump at people's feet. You don't get what it's like to have to be careful; you don't get that it matters how people see you.

Amber   I never stop thinking about how other people see me.

Tom   I know I have to calm down but I can't. And I can't hide. Holy fuck, there is just nowhere to hide! I can't have any body but this one; I can't be anybody but who I am—this man in the world who everyone assumes will make a mistake, if they just wait long enough!

And then Diaz is like "both of you sit down! And, Amber, speak ONLY to us and explain what happened next. When you were back in the bed." And Amber, out of breath from fucking me over, is looking at her hands like they're the most fascinating things she's ever seen.

Amber   I don't know how to say out loud what happened next. Which is that I let him do what he wanted. I mean, I lay there as he *pounded* into me, this vacant look in his eyes, just thinking, "you idiot, Amber" because I'd let myself believe that he actually liked me. And also "fuck you, Tom" because stupidly I thought he could see that I'd spent my entire existence feeling ... invisible, and that he would therefore know how amazing it would be just to look at me right now.

And I felt so profoundly, like desperately ... sad, like am I the only one aware of the fact that I'm on this earth, in which case am I really on it? And if I don't exist then who *is* this, what is the point of this brain constantly torturing me with all this self-doubt if there is no self; what is this body I'm inside of, this body I *hate*, that never does what I want it to and doesn't look good in the clothes I put it in, that I don't like to look at too long in the mirror, that seems so wholly inadequate to the task of housing a person in this awful, fucked up world.

And Tom didn't see any of that ... He didn't see or forgive anything of my body or my soul. And I wanted to die.

Tom (*with reluctance*)   Yeah, so.

There are things the body just knows.

Amber (*then, quietly, realizing*)

So of course I didn't say anything else that night. I wasn't even there.

Tom (*quietly, a fear/a discovery*)   So maybe I knew. Maybe I knew. That she wasn't ... And that's the ... That's the thing that I ... I mean, I thought ... Deep down, I thought I was a nice guy.

Amber   But I'm here, now. And I can't just be silent anymore. I can't do that to myself.

Tom   She's crying, all of a sudden, these sort of animal cries that make everyone deeply uncomfortable.

Amber   But the cost of not doing that to myself anymore is ... Tom. Which is just ...

Tom   I don't like seeing her cry like that. It's all just ... It's too much.

Amber   And then *he* starts to cry, and we just …

Amber *and* **Tom**   So now we're both

Tom   sitting there just …

Amber   and Tom is all alone and I wanna …

Tom   I mean there's Amber, and she's gazing at me with this unmistakable … love. Which is like …

Amber   I remember this Kierkegaard quote we learned in Intro Phil. "It belongs to the imperfection of everything human that man can only attain his desire by passing through its opposite."

But I don't know what it means.

Beat.

Tom   Isn't it crazy, the idea that every single thing leads to everything else?

I played the piano for the first time when I was eleven. This was back at 261, when I was in a class with thirty other kids, and none of us paid any attention, just no one did anything anyone told us to, but still this one teacher, Mrs. Landrieu, still she, like found me.

Mrs. Landrieu was sweet and in over her head, like all those kinda offensive movies you see of well-meaning white ladies in inner city schools trying to control this, like, pack of beasts.

But yeah, we probably were a little like beasts. And she *was* sweet. And she was trying. And one day towards the end of a particularly, I mean, a particularly fucked up class—Elijah, who was the worst of the worst and also my best friend—might've implied that he was gonna go to her house and mess her up when he was like, "Mrs. Landrieu, I'm gonna go to your house and mess you up."

And then Mrs. Landrieu, she says in this tiny voice: Elijah, go to the office. Go straight to the principal's office, but here's the thing—he won't go. He just stays there. And the whole class laughs. And this is when she starts to cry.

And the next day, Elijah sits right up front, like an asshole, just to show her who's boss. And yeah, it was funny, but the look on her face like she wanted to die right there on the spot made it not the least bit funny. And so when she calls on me—and I'm telling you her voice has gotten even tinier since yesterday—I'm just like "I think that's a really interesting question, Mrs. Landrieu," which doesn't win me any popularity points but, you know, I see a chance to do something nice for someone and I take it.

That's the kind of guy I thought I was, after all.

Of course she wants to talk to me after class. And I think she's gonna thank me but instead she's like: "Tommy, I wondered if you might like piano lessons."

I'm like "what??" Turns out she teaches piano on the side. So when I show up at her apartment the next day and sit next to her on the piano bench—by the way, I had no interest in the *piano*, zero, but I would also never turn down something that's free—that's like my modus fucking operandi—when I sit next to her and she says really gently and really kindly, "I know your father left a few months ago" I just … I break down.

I mean, I didn't even like the guy. I didn't even like the guy.

And … after that, like … what else can you do. So you just play.

Suddenly they are in a scene—the college party that took place the night of the incident. **Tom** *is agitated and irritable. They have to shout a bit to be heard over the music in the quad.*

Amber (*waving awkwardly at him*)   Tom!

Tom   Sorry—I got a little held up.

Amber   That's totally fine. I've only been here …

She looks at her watch—she's been here forever already.

Like, yeah, not very long.

She holds herself, shivering.

Tom (*annoyed*)   You're cold?

Amber   I'm always cold.

He rolls his eyes.

Tom   You want a drink?

Amber   Like from, the, um, keg?

Tom   Yeah.

Amber   Well, it's so delicious, I don't know how anyone could turn it down.

Tom (*peeved*)   Is that a joke or something?

Amber   Are you okay?

Tom (*angrily*)   Yeah I'm just trying to figure out if you want a beer. Is that okay by you?

Amber   You don't seem like you're in the best frame of mind tonight.

Tom   Who talks that way: "the best frame of mind"?

Amber   I do.

Tom   I know. It's weird.

Amber   Is it?

Tom   We could also just get outta here.

Amber   Sure.

I mean, we could go inside and like, dance. Or find another party. Or get someone to go to Varsity and pick stuff up for us.

Tom   Why would we do that when there are free drinks right here.

Amber   Good point. We wouldn't. I'm just happy to do what you want to do.

Tom   I'm gonna get a beer for the road.

Amber   I also have a, um.

She pulls out her flask.

Heather got it for me.

Tom   Heather's the hot one, right?

Amber   I mean, yes, she is very attractive. Like, objectively attractive. She has a lot of qualities men would find attractive, I guess. Like she has a very nice body—

Tom   Can I just … Lemme just see that flask.

He drinks from it; she drinks from it; this relaxes him.

That's good. What is that?

Amber   I'm not sure because Heather just gave it to me so …

Tom   It's tequila.

Amber   If you knew, why'd you ask?

Tom (*smiling*)   Maybe I was testing you.

Amber   Why would you be doing that?

Tom   See if you're up to my super high standards.

Amber   From what I hear you have no standards at all.

Tom   Now who told you that.

Amber   I think there's a whole website at Princeton devoted to it.

Tom (*dry*)   That's hilarious.

Amber   I thought so.

Tom   What can I say? I like women. That's not a crime.

Amber   No it's not.

Tom   And I like you.

Amber (*out of awkwardness at being complimented*)   So, how much do you know about the pratfall effect?

Tom   What?

Amber   I was reading about it tonight in our psych book and it's actually really interesting: it's about how a person's attractiveness increases or decreases after he or she makes a mistake. So a highly-competent person, like, say, a celebrity, would be *more* likable after committing a blunder, while the opposite would be true if—

Tom   God, do you ever stop talking?

Amber   What?

Tom (*with a small smile*)   Just stop talking.

Amber   Okay.

Tom   I'm gonna kiss you now.

Amber   Oh.

Okay.

He does; it's actually kinda tender. When it's over, **Amber** *doesn't know what to say.*

Amber   Let's play a game. Let's play Two Truths and a Lie.

Tom   Um. No.

Amber   Come on.

Tom   Okay. I have two truths for you … I hate games and I hate that game.

Amber   But you'll play it.

Tom   And why would I do that?

Amber (*slower and more pointed than the first time around*)   If you wanna sleep with me tonight, for one thing.

Tom (*slower and less of a joke than the first time around*)   Who goes first?

A light gray feather falls from above, right in between **Amber** *and* **Tom**. *Before it hits the ground—blackout.*

End of play

Another Way Home

Another Way Home received its world premiere on November 13, 2012 at Magic Theatre, San Francisco, CA. (Loretta Greco, Producing Artistic Director).

Director: Meredith McDonough

Cast

Lillian	**Kim Martin-Cotten**
Phillip	**Mark Pinter**
Joey	**Daniel Petzold**
Nora	**Riley Krull**
Mike T.	**Jeremy Kahn**

Dramaturg	Carrie Hughes
Stage Manager	Angela Nostrand
Scenic and Costume	Annie Smart
Lighting	Paul Toben
Sound	Sara Huddleston

Opening night November 13, 2012 at the Magic Theatre (San Francisco)

Development of Another Way Home *was supported by the Eugene O'Neill Theater Center during a residency at the National Playwrights Conference of 2011. Preston Whiteway, Executive Director; Wendy Goldberg, Artistic Director.*

Developed as part of Chautauqua Theater Company's New Play Workshop series, 2010.

The play was a recipient of an Edgerton Foundation New American Plays Award.

Characters

Philip—*Jewish, upper middle class, in his fifties, married to* **Lillian**
Lillian—*Jewish, upper middle class, in her forties, married to* **Philip**
Joey—**Lillian** *and* **Philip**'s *sixteen-year-old son*
Nora—**Lillian** *and* **Philip**'s *fifteen-year-old daughter*
Mike T.—**Joey**'s *camp counselor, early-mid twenties*

Time: *2010 or thereabout*

Note on the text: "Beat" and "Breath" both signify pauses in the action. A breath is a shorter beat.

Lillian *and* **Philip** *address the audience.*

Philip   It was … well, it was quite a weekend.

Lillian   We were visiting him at sleep-away camp, up in Maine.

Philip   Our son, she means our son.

Lillian   Joseph. Well, Joey. He goes by Joey now even though we named him Joseph. Or what were the other things they were calling him?

Philip   J-dog. J-Nay.

Lillian   I might never understand it.

Philip   Our last name is Nadelman, so Joey Nadelman—J-Nay. I think it's got a kind of pleasing … folksiness. An intimacy. I wouldn't mind if my partners called me P-Nay.

Lillian   Yes. You would.

Philip   Anyway—there we were, at Kickapoo—

Lillian   Camp Kickapoo. Which means …

She looks at him; he shrugs.

Well, it must mean something.

Philip   It was our fourth summer going to visiting day up in Sweden, Maine.

Lillian   Sweden, Maine—as though an entire Scandinavian country full of fjords and yodelers could fit into this strange bi-partisan state.

Philip   Really, Lily—yodelers? And Maine's not really bi-partisan. They just don't like *anyone*, certainly not *us*, except for the fact that we fill the sleep-away camps and on weekends like this the inns and B&Bs, and are even willing to wear those absurd lobster bibs when we go to nice restaurants—*nice* restaurants—in Maine!

Lillian   Philip.

Philip   Lillian.

Lillian   Anyway. We flew to Portland.

Philip   Sometimes we drove, but this time we flew.

Lillian   Philip had been working so hard that week and I could tell he was tired. The bags under his eyes. My god. Sometimes, when he's working hard, I worry he'll just keel over. Just like that. Dead. It's the worst thing I can think of happening.

Philip (*playfully*)   Except when she's mad at me. When Lillian's angry with me, she's been known to say things like: "Philip, just die, why don't you."

Lillian   He's joking.

Philip (*considering it*)   No I'm not.

Lillian (*whispering conspiratorially with the audience*)   He is.

Philip   I slept on the plane. It had been a long week. I really shouldn't have gone at all—my partners were in the office that weekend—but this was my boy, this was Joseph.

Lillian (*baffled by the nickname*)   Our little *J-dog*.

Philip   So when we got to Sweden in our rental convertible—

Lillian   I *hate* convertibles, but Philip deserves his toys, I suppose—

Philip   When we got there, we easily found the little road off the main road that takes you to the little road to Joey's camp.

Lillian   It was a scorchingly hot day. I tried to call Susan to get out of hosting next week's book club brunch but there was no reception. AT&T, so what do you expect.

Philip   I said: maybe we should focus on Joseph instead of making phone calls.

Lillian   I said: we're not there yet. Furthermore, I don't think you should lecture me on time spent focusing on Joseph.

Philip   I said: what is that supposed to mean?

Lillian   And it was the usual fight—this time in the scorching heat.

Philip   By the time we arrived, by the time we pulled under the wooden banner—Camp Kickapoo!—we were sweating as though we were in some African desert. The sweat slid into my ears so I could barely hear myself cursing my wife.

Lillian   Just shut up, I said. I said shut up, shut up, shut up.

Philip   She did; she did say that.

Lillian   Our boy will hear us.

Philip   And sure enough, as they were every summer on this particular day, the boys were lined up waiting for the cars as they pulled in.

Joey enters.

Lillian   Joseph smiled casually upon seeing us. He was a CIT this year—

Philip   Counselor in training—

Lillian   Which meant he was practically an adult but also not one at all. He smiled casually, as though we'd seen him two hours ago and were merely dropping off something he left behind.

Philip   "Joseph," I called out to him. "Joey." I parked the car.

Lillian   Oh come here, come here. It's so good to see you!

She envelops him. He squirms away.

Philip   J-dog. Give your old man a hug.

Joey   Hey.

Philip   No hug?

Beat.

Why don't you gimme some skin.

Nothing. **Philip**'s *left hanging.*

Lillian   Joseph, Joseph, Joseph.

Joey   Joey. (Beat) Joey Joey Joey.

Lillian   Joey isn't your name.

Joey   It is.

Lillian   Anyway, we're so happy to see you.

Breath.

Philip (*to the audience*)   Joey isn't an easy kid. We love him; we cherish him, but he isn't an easy kid.

Lillian   Lots of learning "issues." Lots of social "issues." First they said it was ADD, then ADHD, then autism. Then it was a mood disorder, then an anxiety disorder, then oppositional defiant disorder, and most recently: depression. His diagnoses change as much as he does. I hope that means that maybe he's just … growing up.

Philip   Really?

Lillian   What do you mean: "really"?

Philip   Some of us are ready to let him grow up. Some of us aren't constantly …

Lillian   Well, sometimes one *should* worry, Philip. I mean, some things one shouldn't be *able* to simply accept. Like at school, Joseph sits alone at lunch. He has no friends.

Philip   Because he's angry. Above all, he's angry, seems angry to be in the world, put upon.

Lillian   We can't do anything about it, and it breaks our hearts.

Breath.

Philip   But at camp, it was different. At Kickapoo, the boys gave him nicknames, which is a form of acceptance, isn't it? There was a chant about him, which we overheard once. How'd it go?

Lillian   Joey, Joey, he's our man. If he can do it, anyone can.

Breath.

Philip   It wasn't nice, necessarily, but it meant he was being noticed. He was here … So Kickapoo was important. It was important.

Lillian (*to* **Joey**)   Have you gotten my letters, sweetheart?

Joey *shrugs.*

Lillian   You don't know, or you don't care to answer?

He shrugs again.

Lillian (*sweetly*)   You know, I work hard on those letters. It takes me time to write them every day.

Joey   Why are you questioning me about the fucking letters??!

Philip   Please apologize to your mother.

Joey   I didn't ask her to write them!

Lillian   How hard would it be to ever thank me for anything?

Joey   Hard.

Philip   You've just gotta loosen up, J-man. Lighten up. The world isn't so awful.

Joey   Yes. It is.

Beat.

Philip   So how's color war going?

Lillian   Oh yes—is blue gonna win this year?

Joey   Mom.

Lillian (*to the audience*)   At Kickapoo, color war went on all summer. You were assigned a team your first summer at the camp and then you were on that team for the rest of your time there, for the rest of your life, really.

Philip   Joey actually got pretty into it. Though, there were some instances of slightly aggressive behavior on his part … (**Lillian** *glares at him*) Which are not actually worth mentioning.

Joey   If you really must know, blue sucks this year. We're gonna lose. So thanks for bringing it up, mom.

Philip   She's trying to be friendly.

Joey   She's trying too hard.

Lillian (*trying to contain her annoyance*)   Okay. Well. I'd like to use the little girl's room.

Joey   I hate when you call it that.

Lillian   Is there anything I *am* permitted to say?

Philip   Go easy on your mother. It's incredibly hot. I forced her to ride in a BMW convertible.

Joey   Poor Mom.

Lillian   Have you been using sunscreen?

Joey   No.

Lillian   I didn't think so. You're all red. Joseph, you must put on lotion. You must.

Joey   Or what?

Lillian   Or you'll get cancer like Grandpa.

Joey   But he didn't die.

Lillian   Is the only reason to do something to avoid death?

Joey   Yes.

Lillian   That's ridiculous. (*Looking at* **Philip**.) Philip.

Philip   Yes?

Lillian   Don't you think Joseph should wear sunscreen?

Philip (*half-heartedly*)   I do. I think you should wear sunscreen.

Lillian (*to* **Philip**)   Why do you do this?

Philip   Do what?

Lillian   Joseph, you can't stay here if you don't take care of yourself. We'll bring you back with us. I mean, look at you. Look at him, Philip. He's all red.

Philip   It's six weeks. Whatever doesn't kill us makes us stronger, right J-dog?

Lillian   Until it kills you.

Joey   I'm not afraid of death.

Breath.

Lillian   All right. I'm going to find a bathroom.

She exits. An awkward beat.

Philip   So, J-Nay, how goes it?

Joey *doesn't respond.*

Are you doing okay?

Joey   Sure.

Philip   Playing a lot of tennis?

Joey   Some.

Philip   You higher on the ladder than last summer?

Joey *doesn't say anything.*

Not that it matters. It doesn't matter. It's all about enjoying yourself. It's about …

Joey   What's it about, Dad?

Philip   How are … Sam? Is it Sam? And Jeremy?

Joey   They're fine.

Philip   Are they in your bunk?

Joey   I'm a CIT.

Philip   So?

Joey   So I don't live in a bunk with the other CITs. We each have a different bunk. We're, like, counselors.

Philip   Oh, right. And are you enjoying that?

Beat.

Joey   Sure.

Philip   It's all about enjoying it. About getting something out of it. That's all it's about.

Beat.

Joey   How are things at work?

Philip   Oh, good. Good … Always lots to do. Too much to do.

Joey   But you're enjoying it?

Philip   What?

Joey   The work. That's what it's all about, right? Enjoying it?

Philip   Oh. Well, no. Not really.

Joey   That's not what it's all about or you're not enjoying it?

Philip   You can't expect to enjoy work. It's not summer-camp. That's the difference between work and summer-camp.

Joey   So I better really enjoy summer-camp before my life turns to shit.

Philip   That's not what I'm saying.

Joey   Then what are you saying?

Philip   I don't know … Just that … it's exciting, being young. Once you're old like me, you don't do anything for the first time. It's the same thing every day … Go to the office, come home … You know, there's a routine.

A change in tone. **Joey** *softens.*

Joey   When I get home, maybe I'll come to the office with you one day. The way I did when I was a kid.

Beat.

Philip   That'd be really nice.

Joey   Everyone knew me there. Everyone was happy to see me. The secretaries. Your partners.

Philip   That's true.

Joey   And the views of the city were amazing. I remember just sitting in your office, not doing anything, just staring out the window.

Philip   Do you?

Joey   Yeah.

Philip   I remember it too.

Joey   I would just sit there while you worked.

Philip   I remember.

Joey   Dad?

Philip   Yeah, kiddo.

Joey   I'm not sure I want to come back here next summer.

Philip   Well, you don't have to. If you're not having fun, there's no reason to—

Joey   I am having fun. I just …

Philip   You don't have to come back, Joey.

Lillian *returns.*

Lillian   I didn't go. It was an outhouse. I waited in line and then I realized it was an outhouse!

Philip (*annoyed*)   So you didn't go?

Lillian   I did run into that counselor, though. The tennis director?

Philip   The handsome one. The one you always manage to run into?

Lillian   Now that you mention it, he is quite handsome.

Joey   Terrific.

Lillian Is he Mexican? Or … Filipino? I mean, you just can't tell with some people. But he has the most lovely piercing eyes. As though he could see right through all the bullshit. A little like President Obama, actually.

Joey Mom.

Philip Your mother is easily taken in by appearances and empty rhetoric.

Lillian Stop it, Philip.

Philip Remember when she developed a crush on that curator at the Met? We had to join the Met just so she could go listen to him give these talks. Was your mother really interested in ancient Greek urns? I don't think so.

Lillian I believe you're referring to vases, which were actually called amphora. And I happened to like them very much—each amphora told a beautiful story. And there was nothing empty about Paul's discussions. They were very fulfilling. Very enlightening.

Philip What could talking about ancient Greek pottery have to do with your life?

Lillian Everything, Philip. It had everything to do with my life. My life is emptier without those talks.

Philip Then fill it.

Lillian Don't say that.

Beat.

Philip Why don't we go to your bunk, Joey.

Joey You don't want to see my bunk. It's disgusting. You'll just get upset.

Lillian I'll try to take it in stride.

Joey No. Why can't you ever take me seriously? I said no.

Philip You can't say no to your parents. If you want to tell your friends no, if you want to be rude to them, that's your business, but you can't act that way with us. No way buster. Not a chance.

Lillian (*adding to the problem for* **Joey** *was that …*) Another thing was how *great* Joseph's sister was. His little sister Nora.

Philip Nora. Ruth. Nadelman.

She enters, with books under her arm, and wearing glasses.

A name that could sit on the Supreme Court. A girl who aced her PSATs, who gets 5s on all her APs, whose teachers rave about her—

Lillian Fight over her—

Philip This year the debate advisor called to get us to persuade Nora to do debate instead of Model Congress. But it wasn't up to us.

Lillian Anyway, this girl, this amazing girl, who seems incapable of failing—

Philip Who confirms we're not complete fuck-ups as parents—

Lillian This girl who can persuade anyone of anything, is somehow—

Philip Well, she's fascinated by—

Lillian Obsessed with—

Philip This incredibly … leggy pop star — I mean you should see her—

Lillian Enough with her legs.

Philip *and* **Lillian** Taylor Swift.

Nora *lets down her hair, takes off her glasses, and sings a portion of Taylor Swift's "Love Story" in a good impersonation of the singer.*

Nora
> *And I said,*
> *"Romeo, take me somewhere we can be alone.*
> *I'll be waiting, all that's left to do is run.*
> *You be the prince, and I'll be the princess,*
> *It's a love story, baby, just say, 'yes'."*

Nora *exits.*

Lillian I mean, isn't it amazing how these strangers enter our homes?

Philip Our lives?

*The lights shift. In **Joey**'s bunk.*

Lillian That bathroom is disgusting. Doesn't anyone ever clean it?

Joey We don't have maids here, Mom.

Mike The boys are supposed to do it.

Lillian (*noticing* **Mike**) Oh hello.

Mike But they don't really do it. Joey and I end up cleaning them, which we kinda resent, but it's tough to hard-core resent eight-year-olds. Right, Joey?

Mike *holds out his fist for a fist bump but Joey ignores him.*

Joey What are you doing here?

Mike It's good to see you too, J-dog.

Joey Why aren't you at lunch?

Mike (*light, breezy*) Well, I was hoping to meet your parents.

Joey No. You can't meet them.

Lillian Of course he can. We're right here. Hi—I'm Lillian.

Philip *sticking out his hand to be slapped.*

Philip Nadelman. But you can call me P-Nay.

Mike (*weirded out, but slapping his hand*) Okay.

Joey (*with hostility, to his parents*) This is Mike T.

Philip Mike T. Is that a nickname?

Joey (*annoyed*) No. There's another Mike in the bunk. Mike M.

Lillian Are you another CIT?

Joey No.

Mike I'm the counselor.

Lillian Oh, I'm sorry—

Mike Don't worry about it. I'm not that much older than Joey, so.

Lillian Joseph.

Joey Mom.

Philip So how many summers have you been at Kickapoo then?

Joey This is his first one. And maybe his last. Can we go now?

Lillian Joseph, that's awfully impolite.

Mike   It's okay. And yeah … it's my first time here. My first time at camp, actually.

Lillian   It's so American, don't you think?

Mike   What do you mean by that?

Lillian   My mother was Polish, originally, and she was always so baffled by the idea of camp. She'd say "why would you want to go live in the woods when you can live in a house, with plumbing and heating?"

Mike   Sounds like a smart lady.

Lillian   Well if you don't have much you don't understand why anyone would ever willingly give anything up. When I was a girl, my mother saved every magazine, every paper bag—

Philip   Every ketchup packet. Every piece of mail she ever received. Every ticket stub.

Lillian   She was a bit of a hoarder, it's true.

Philip   A bit.

Lillian   Philip.

Philip   The bottom line is: you work hard to give your children what you didn't have yourself. I never went to camp.

Lillian   And Kickapoo is just so beautiful. I love coming up here, getting to be in the middle of nature.

Joey   That's why you avoid the outdoors whenever you're here, right Mom? Because you love it so much.

Lillian   You can appreciate the outdoors from indoors, I've always said. I mean, the view from Kickapoo's lodge all the way down to the lake is breathtaking. Truly, the camp looks just like its brochure. Sometimes a place doesn't look at all like its brochure.

Joey (*under his breath*)   Sometimes a person isn't at all who he seems.

They don't hear him.

Lillian   So … do you have brothers and sisters, Mike? Or is all of this a bit of a shock to you?

Joey   He has three sisters. Please can we go?

Lillian   Three sisters, my heavens.

Joey   But they annoy him.

Philip   That's the nice thing about camp, isn't it? Getting a new family for a little while, right? We know Joey prefers it to his own family—right, kiddo?

Joey   Pretty much.

Awkward beat.

Mike   So … you must be exhausted. All that driving … All the way from New York.

Lillian   Actually, we flew. Philip had too much work for us to leave yesterday. Though I would have liked to.

Philip   Philip's *work* is what allows you to lead the life of comfort and luxury you take for granted every day.

Lillian   Philip!

Breath.

Mike   It's funny. Meeting you two.

Philip   Why's that?

Joey   Don't. Please don't be an asshole right now, okay?

Mike   Joey, I'm not sure what's …

Joey   Oh you're not sure?

Lillian   You know—no wonder you have trouble … forming connections, Joseph.

Joey   Excuse me??

Philip   At least he's talking.

Joey   I'm right here!

Philip   He didn't say a word in the week or so before he left for camp. We thought maybe he was preparing himself for how hard it would be not to be able to talk to us every day.

Joey   Maybe I needed a break from your abuse.

Lillian   Abuse!

Joey   I mean, what are you trying to do to me?

Lillian *steps forward into a pool of light;* **Joey** *and* **Mike** *both listen to her letter, though* **Joey** *seems to find listening to it almost physically painful. He turns around so he's not facing* **Lillian** *midway through.*

Lillian

June 16th

Dear Joseph, you only left this morning but already I miss you. I went on a walk in the park and I saw this boy, who, from a distance, might have been you. And I sped up to him, only to realize he was nothing like you at all. I'll blame the sunlight, which was very bright. Later, I went to Gristedes' and got the fixings for chicken cacciatore. I think I'll make it tonight because it's your father's favorite. Hopefully he'll be home this evening. I feel like I never see him these days. But you know he misses you too, even though he doesn't come out and tell you so. Just not his way, I guess. But I look at the photos I took just after you were born and the way he gazes at you is just ... well, I don't think he's ever been so in love ... Anyway—I'm sure you're already totally ensconced. Just don't forget to smile at people—that tells them that you like them and that they can talk to you. And don't forget to shower. I know last summer you had a lot of other stuff going on, but it is important, Joseph. And take your Claritin. And your Ritalin. And your Lexapro. Just stop by the infirmary every morning on the way to breakfast. Make it part of your routine. And ... smile. Be friendly. Don't tell people you hate them. You are my pride and joy. Go Mets! Love, Mom.

Joey   I mean, have you thought of that? Maybe I don't want to know what you're thinking all the time. Maybe I'm all the way in Maine because I wanted to be far away, in the middle of fucking nowhere.

Philip   On second thought, maybe it was better when he *wasn't* talking.

Lillian   Philip!

Mike   So I don't know if Joey told you but I'm directing the upper camp play and I've been trying to get him to audition ... We're doing this abridged version of Stoppard's Coast of Utopia.

Joey   Just stop talking, Mike. God.

Mike   Joey, what is your problem today??

Lillian   See! Your father and I are not the problem, Joseph.

Joey   Who knows? Who knows? It's too bad my life couldn't be some huge science experiment where we could see if I'd turn out different if I was raised by different parents. Parents I don't fucking hate.

Lillian   Why are you being so cruel, honey? Did something happen to you?

Joey   You guys happened to me. Okay? You guys.

Philip   That's it. I've had it.

Joey (*to* **Mike**)   Now's when he blows up and acts like an asshole.

Philip   You've been nothing but a little prick since the moment we got here. You don't know the pile of work I have waiting for me back home. You don't know what I gave up to be here.

Joey   But I didn't ask you to come! I didn't even want you to come! Most of the other CITs' parents aren't here. They're, like, busy treating their kids like fucking adults. I didn't ask you to come!

Philip   No, you certainly didn't. You wouldn't do anything that resembled what a normal … I mean, your sister liked it when we visited her at camp. She made us feel good for having made the trip.

Joey   Well, I'm really sorry.

Philip   No you're not. You're not at all sorry. So just get lost, will you?

Joey   You're kicking me out of my own bunk?

Philip   Oh! Your bunk? This is my bunk, kiddo.

Lillian   Okay, Philip—

Philip   Did you apply for this job? Are you being paid a wage? No. So who paid for you to be here? Whose bunk is this? That's right. You don't have a leg to stand on, Joseph. This isn't a real job. You're not a real counselor. Not an adult, either, just a big child who can't control himself. So go! Just get out of my sight!

Joey *looks at him, hurt. He exits. A long beat.*

Lillian (*quietly*)   Philip, do something … Go after him.

Philip   I will not.

Mike   I'll get him, if you want.

Philip   No—let him simmer down.

Lillian (*to* **Philip**)   More like let you simmer down.

Philip   Excuse me?

Lillian   I'm so sorry you had to see that. Philip can be …

Philip   Me??

Lillian   Yes, you. You lose it sometimes. I'm not saying Joseph doesn't … provoke it.

He does.

Philip   He's an infuriating kid. You can't punish him; he weasels out of it. You can't incentivize him because he doesn't care. I mean, if I said to my father even half the things he said to me, my father would have actually killed me.

Lillian (*under her breath*)   Your father was a psychopath.

Philip   That's not true.

Lillian   No?

Philip   Our own little Holden Caulfield. I mean, what the hell is wrong with him? We just came all the way here …

Mike   I don't know what's going on today. He's not usually like that.

Breath.

I mean, I'd heard that he could be a little difficult but we get along fine. He's been great.

Philip   He has?

Lillian   Oh is that good to hear … So … does that mean that … ?

Breath.

Philip   She wants you to elaborate.

Lillian   I'm sorry. You've probably never been a source of real worry to anyone. You're so cool and hip and in.

Mike (*laughing*)   Oh, no. Not at all.

Lillian   No? But you seem … You look …

Mike   What do I look like to you?

Philip   I think Lillian just meant that you seem very together. Which is true of most people, compared to our son.

Lillian   And you have interests. Didn't you say you're directing the play?

Mike   I'm the drama counselor here, yeah.

... Do you, um, do you like theater?

Lillian   Oh I love it.

Mike   You do?

Philip   When's the last time you saw a play, Lillian?

Lillian   I see plays ... I saw that one with the fellow from the TV show in it.

Philip   I'm sure that could describe almost any play in New York.

Lillian We took Nora and Joseph to see *Wicked* a few years ago and then had to spend as much on merchandise as we had on the ticket. Nora had to have everything—the shirt, the poster, the *tote bag.*

Mike   Joey didn't want anything?

Philip   What do you think?

Mike   I think Joey isn't into wanting what other people want. That's what I like about him.

Beat as **Lillian** *happily takes this in.*

Lillian   So why drama? What got you into it?

Mike   Well, part of this summer is to see how into it I really am. I know it's not the most practical thing to do.

Philip   All the better, according to my wife.

Mike   But it's the first thing I've really *liked*, you know? That when I think about the future maybe I could see myself doing.

Lillian   That's exciting, isn't it?

Mike   Yeah ... it is.

I mean, I don't know if I'm any good at it. In tenth grade, I just, I pulled a hamstring and I couldn't play basketball. And there was this girl who was auditioning for the play—

Philip   It's always a girl, isn't it.

Lillian   Right, Philip. Name three instances in your life when you changed your mind because of a girl.

Philip   Okay. I went to Harvard because Caren Pfizer was going to Stanford and I wanted to be as far away from her as I possibly could; I took driver's ed for a second time because I was too distracted the first time around by Peggy Goldsmith's décolletage, which might I add was really something; I applied to clerk for the Second Circuit because the love of my life was moving to New York no matter what, even though I told her I thought our lives would be better elsewhere. Easier. And now she's angry with me for having the kind of job one has to have to survive in New York. Go figure.

Lillian   The love of your life.

Philip (*grudgingly*)   That'd be you, Lil. As much as you try to deny it.

A breath.

Lillian (*quietly, in awe*)   How on earth do you remember all of that?

Philip (*wistful*)   … It's more that you forget all the rest.

Mike   I know. I feel like I remember the weirdest things.

Philip (*dryly*)   Well, you *should* remember everything. Your memory banks aren't corroded yet.

Mike   I remember Joey told me you were a great photographer.

Lillian   He didn't really say that, did he?

Mike   He did.

Lillian   Gosh, that's funny. Especially because it's not true.

Philip   It is true. She takes the most incredible photographs of our children. Or she used to.

Lillian   That's not really being a photographer.

Philip (*kindly, generously*)   And she has a portfolio. And it's gorgeous, a gorgeous portfolio, full of … what would you call them? Like urban landscapes and street scenes; she loved New York back then. And she used to have her stuff in galleries. I was so proud of her. But she hasn't taken a photograph in years now.

Lillian   Philip.

Philip   I wish she would.

Lillian   If I did, who would spend any time with our children?

Mike   … you know, you have a really great family. From what I hear.

Philip   Oh yes we're terribly proud.

Mike   No—I'm serious.

Lillian (*to the audience*)   And somehow when he said it, I believed it. For a moment.

Philip (*to the audience*)   He looked at her—at my wife—so tenderly. So gently that I actually wondered when the last time was when I looked at her like that. And I couldn't remember.

Beat.

Lillian (*gently*)   Philip, where are you? Where have you gone?

Long beat.

Philip   We should find him, don't you think?

Beat.

Lillian   Yes. I think we should. (*To the audience.*) And then things happened quickly.

Philip   Because we went looking for Joey. And we couldn't find him.

Lillian   We looked everywhere.

Philip   We asked everyone.

Lillian   And no one had seen him.

Philip   We stood on the soccer field in the fading daylight, and I swear I almost saw him there …

Lillian   But as a little boy. The way, when he played soccer he would stay in one place as the ball went past him, jumping up and down from the excitement of it all.

Philip (*correcting her, with some frustration*)   Except he isn't a little boy anymore, and he wasn't on the soccer field.

Lillian   So we moved on.

Philip   We looked for him everywhere, and after a few hours, all the cars in the parking lot had left for the day.

Lillian   All the other parents had returned to their inns or motels or B&Bs and were now having a drink at the bar, or sitting out on the porch, rhapsodizing about how great it was to see little Jimmy, how much he'd grown.

Philip   While we were left here, our car all alone in the shadows, a little like the way our child goes through his life.

They exit. **Nora** *enters, emailing. A flashback.*

Nora   Dear Joey, I think maybe I keep emailing you because the more I write the more ridiculous it is that you're not writing back, and someday I can say, "Can you believe I sent him 11 emails and three New Yorker cartoon app e-cards and never heard a thing?" And people will feel sorry for me. Or for you.

Anyway, I'm sorry I can't come up to Maine with Mom and Dad this weekend, but someone has to walk Mrs. Dalloway and I guess that someone is me. Not that I'm psyched to stay alone. Remember that time we thought someone had broken in and we hid in your room but then it turned out it was just the mop had fallen over? That was so crazy. I guess I should have gone away this summer too. But I thought I could just read and tutor poor kids and study for the SATs and listen to Taylor, who by the way is also so impressive just as a person—I mean, the way she took on the streaming services and totally promoted the value of *art*? She's just, like, amazing. Anyway, I thought I'd take walks and stuff and be alone, but now I realize that being alone is … well, lonely.

Or maybe I'm writing because I'm totally effing bored. Or maybe because after my SAT tutor leaves, I walk by your room and it feels really empty. And the fact that you have absolutely nothing on your walls freaks me out even more when you're not here, because it makes me think you've like died or something. I mean, with all my friends away this summer, I was thinking that I feel a little like you must feel all the time. And it doesn't feel good.

I miss you. xoxo, Nora.

Joey *emails her back—also in the past.*

Joey   Hi, Nora. So I bet you're shocked to see my name in your inbox. So, surprise! Here I am. Your brother Joey, away at camp, writing you for the first time ever. Because it's weird. Being a counselor. Or a sort of counselor. I've never had anyone, like, look up to me. And these kids are total fucking dweebs but they do kinda look up to me. Sometimes I even make them laugh. Mike T.—the counselor in the bunk—says I have a very natural sense of humor, and no one has ever told me I had a natural anything, and so I feel a little … I don't know. And he likes my cow shirt too—you know, my t-shirt with the cow on it and the little bubble that says "I'm not interested in any bull"? He thinks it's funny. He's very … He's like really nice to me; even on the first day he was nice to me. And he majors in Drama at Vassar, and one night he told me about this acting class he took on empathy and how empathy is like all you need to be a good actor, and also like, a good person, and I was like: I don't think so; I think it takes more than some stupid acting technique to be a good person, but I don't know, I was thinking maybe I'll go to Vassar even though dad once said "isn't that all women?" even though it's been co-ed for like forty years or something. Sometimes dad really lives in the past. Also: I fucking hate A-Rod. He is the most overpaid cheater in the history of any sport, even taking inflation into account. Asshole.

Nora   Joey—I was so happy to get your email! I was actually really, really surprised. I even told Roberto, this kid I was tutoring today, how happy I was to hear from you, and he said "why doesn't your brother write you more often, if it makes you so happy?" and I said "Roberto, maybe he doesn't know how happy it makes me so I better tell him." So here I am telling you how happy it made me. Please write again! Tell me what you're up to, what you do every day. xoxo Nora

Joey   Dear Nora. Fuck you.

They exit. **Philip** *and* **Lillian** *enter.*

Philip   We kept looking, and soon the camp was looking for him too.

Lillian   We circled the lodge, inside and out. Joseph? We called out to him. Joseph?

Philip   We checked down at the lake. It was deserted, except for two counselors on the beach, carrying canoes down to the shore, their heads obscured by the boats, inside the boats, so it looked like the canoes were walking themselves down to the water.

Lillian   Like canoes made out of men, and the whole world upside down.

Philip   We looked on the tennis courts. And the basketball courts. We walked around the soccer field twice. We went into the yurt by the campfire, which seemed like a good place for a boy to hide, or to bring a girl during a social. But he wasn't there.

Lillian   The whole camp was swarming with people, looking for him, and I thought, sadly, despite myself, that our son had never been so popular.

Breath.

Philip   We were walking across the meadow in the near-dark and Lillian's shoes began to hurt her. Somehow she's never in the right shoes. Even her sneakers give her blisters. And as she was leaning on my shoulder so she could apply another useless band-aid to her ailing feet, I glanced at a bird winging its way across the twilit Maine sky and realized I'd been alive fifty-eight years. I'd been alive fifty-eight years and I had no idea where they went. I had a wife and two children and an apartment and a decent job, and I was hardly a part of any of it. It was one of those realizations. I was fifty-*eight* years old.

Lillian   I found some service! Can you believe that?? We should call Nora.

Philip   Now?

Lillian   What if she heard from Joseph?

Philip   Okay, but don't make her too nervous. Your forte is needlessly worrying people.

Lillian   Thank you, Philip, for your generous assessment of my strengths and weaknesses.

Lillian *dials.* **Nora** *enters, her cell phone ringing its Taylor Swift ringtone. She answers.*

Nora   Hi Mom.

Lillian   Hi sweetie. What are you doing?

Nora   Same thing I was doing when you called this morning. Nothing.

Lillian   I don't like when you say you're doing nothing.

Nora   Why?

Lillian   You should be doing something. You're … young, sweetheart. You should do things.

Nora   What are you doing?

Lillian   Well … we're standing in a very beautiful meadow.

Nora   Excellent. I'm sitting in my very small bedroom.

Lillian It's not so small.

Philip Tell her *she's* pretty small. She doesn't need a big room.

Nora If I sit on the bed, I can touch both walls.

Lillian You're pretty small, Nora-bear.

Nora Please don't demean me. How's Joey?

Lillian Oh, he's fine.

Nora (*suspiciously*) Really?

Lillian Really, he is.

Nora Are people making fun of him?? Is it like that time when cousin Nick said Joey was self-important and he thought he was calling him impotent and he like flew into a rage?

Lillian No. No, it's not that at all. It's just there was this silly … incident.

Nora What happened?

Philip *indicates that she not tell her.*

Lillian No, it was nothing. It was silly. He and your father had a fight—

Philip *signals wildly that she stop; she ignores him.*

And now he's sort of … taken off.

Nora What do you mean "taken off"?

Lillian Just what it sounds like.

Nora Like he ran away?

Lillian It looks like it.

Beat.

Nora (*freaking out*) Ohmygod.

Philip Is she freaking out?

Nora It's actually happening. This is what I've always worried would happen and it's happening.

Lillian What?

Nora   I always worried he would hurt himself. That he'd climb to the top of some building and jump off and then we'd have to live with the guilt of how sad he really must have been.

Lillian   Don't say that!

Philip (*taking the phone*)   Gimme that.

He takes the phone.

Nora, it's your dad. I don't want you to worry, okay?

Nora   Have they dragged the lake?

Philip   What? Drag the lake? No. Of course not.

Lillian   Oh god, should they drag the lake?

He puts his hand over the mouthpiece and says to **Lillian**.

Philip   No.

Nora   Dad?

Philip   I should probably go.

Nora   You can't just go. I can't just sit here.

Philip   Why don't you …

Lillian   Tell her to try to think of places he might have gone.

Philip   Why don't you think of places he might have gone.

Nora   But Joey's not predictable! That's the only predictable thing about Joey.

Lillian   Tell her to wait by the phone. Maybe he'll call her.

Philip   Wait by the phone because maybe your brother will call you.

Nora   Okay, for one, I am always by my phone because we live in the twenty-first century and we have *mobile* phones, which means we carry them with us; and two: he would never call me. He only just started emailing me, which doesn't involve actually having to have a conversation. He has never once called me on my phone. Let me talk to mom.

He hands **Lillian** *the phone.*

Lillian   Nora?

Nora   Joey said something to me.

Lillian   What? When?

Nora   It was this spring sometime. And you know how he always says stuff like "I wish I were dead" and, like "kill me, now" and stuff like that?

Lillian   Yes, Nora, what's your point?

Philip   What is she saying? Whatever she's saying, don't listen. You two will drive each other nuts.

Nora   He walked into my room, and he sat down on the beanbag, which he never does. He never sits down. But this time he sat and he looked really solemn and he just said, "Nora, when I die, will you take care of Mom and Dad?"

Lillian   He said that?

Nora   Yeah, and I was like "what're you talking about, Joey?" but he just stood up and left. And you know, kids on SSRIs are more prone to suicidal ideation. I've read those studies. There's like a new one in the New York Times every week.

Philip *takes the phone from a stricken* **Lillian**.

Philip   Whatever you're saying, Nora, it's probably not helpful right now. It'll probably just upset your mother.

Nora   I think Joey's scared to grow up.

Philip   Well who isn't, Nora. At your age.

Nora   I'm not.

Philip   Is that really true?

Nora   I mean, think about it: maybe Joey sees his whole life unfolding ahead of him and he doesn't like what he sees. You know, the weird angry kid who turns into a weird angry man, but by that point there's no one to say, "well, it's okay because he's just a kid." At that point he's just *weird* and he won't grow out of it, and he's all alone. So maybe he'd prefer not to face that future.

Philip   I'm hanging up now.

Lillian *takes the phone back.*

Lillian   Joseph really said that, Nora, about "when I die"?

Nora You know, you should really call him Joey. It's how he thinks of himself. And at our age, our identities are really fragile and you have to support their growth into something solid however you can.

Lillian Are we doing that for you? Supporting the growth of your identity?

Nora Find Joey.

Lillian We will.

Nora But if you look for him the way you've looked for a job over the past few years, you'll never find him. Put a little more into it. I don't mean to sound mean.

Lillian You don't mean to sound mean?

Nora No I … I'm sorry. I'm just upset. I'm sorry, mom.

Philip This ends the conversation. And then, Lillian is crying.

She cries a little.

Lillian I'm sorry. I'm just so …

Philip I know.

He holds her.

I know.

She suddenly notices the time.

Lillian Oh my god, can that be right?

Philip What?

Lillian It's been almost ten hours. Philip! Ten.

Philip Okay.

Lillian Okay?

Philip What else can we do but look? And wait.

Lillian Panic. We can panic.

Philip So many people are out looking.

Lillian But we need to do something. We can't just sit here. I can't just wait.

Philip (*to the audience, sadly*)   So we got in our car, in that ridiculous convertible, and kept our eyes out for him as though looking for some animal in the dark, as though he might have turned into something else and escaped, not remembering he was a person, that he was our son, and therefore meant to stay.

Lillian *moves into the spotlight; again* **Mike** *listens to the letter.*

Lillian   June 23rd

Dear Joseph,

Today was another boring old day. Nora locks herself in her room, studying, and your father leaves so early in the morning, so I am left to my own devices, and sometimes, when that happens, life doesn't feel all that meaningful, when you're alone, and thinking about the long drift of time and events.

Then, brightening.

But don't worry about me! That's not for you to do. One day you'll see you were lucky to have two people worrying so much about you. At least I think you will. Not that I can begin to guess what's going on in your head. Even when you were little, I didn't understand you. Sometimes I would pose you for a photograph but by the time I took it you had scampered out of the frame, out of the room. When the picture was developed, I could feel the way you were once there but now gone. But who was that little person? And who was I? And what does a photograph really capture, Joseph? Can it capture the absence of something? Of someone? I think I couldn't take pictures anymore when I finally realized how inadequate they are. That they don't really save anything, and only remind you of everything you don't know.

I'm sorry to blather on. I hope you're wearing your sunscreen and having someone put it on your back where you got so badly burned last summer. In other words, I hope you're having someone watch your back—ha ha. I love you very much, my darling. Mom.

Lights shift. **Philip** *and* **Lillian** *sit tensely in the lodge.*

Philip   The night wore on, and with it grew all these possibilities. They come to you, unbidden:

Lillian   That he's been murdered. That he's hitchhiked with some trucker who ends up twisting Joseph's arm around his back in one of those wrestling moves you see in the movies. That he's in a pool hall trying to hustle people, people he shouldn't be talking to in the first place who couldn't care less about the welfare of some strange misplaced little boy. That he's by the side of the road somewhere. That he's lost. Or that he's not lost and he truly intended to disappear.

Philip   Because *I* …

Lillian   And all of a sudden you start to question everything you thought you knew. Is it possible he really might be a danger to himself? Not that I could say that.

Philip   I couldn't say it. Not out loud. So instead you find yourself saying: There was a time when we were happy, wasn't there?

Lillian   What?

Philip   You heard me.

Lillian   You know, I think we should go to his bunk.

Philip   Someone would have gotten us if he'd shown up there, Lillian.

Lillian   No—to look for clues.

Philip   Clues?

Lillian   Yes, Philip—clues.

Philip (*throwing up his hands*)   Okay we'll go to his bunk.

Lillian   What kinds of things should we look for?

Philip   I don't know. It was your idea!

Lillian   Philip!

Philip   Okay, maybe we'll figure out what was going on. What made him so upset.

Lillian   But *we* were going on. You heard him.

Philip   You don't actually believe that, do you?

Lillian   You just said that you didn't think we were happy anymore.

Philip   So you did hear me.

Lillian   I want to look for clues.

Philip (*grudging*)   We went back to his bunk.

Mike   Any news?

Lillian   No.

Philip   Mike, do you mind if we …

He indicates that they want to look around.

Mike   Of course. Please.

He hands them a flashlight.

Lillian (*to the audience*)   It was certainly an invasion of our son's privacy but it felt justified, given the circumstances. We found his shoebox of stuff and took it outside. Inside were two whistles, a deck of cards, a chewed up pencil, and a *Maxim* magazine.

Philip (*of the magazine*)   Lemme see that.

Lillian   Why does he read this junk?

Philip (*starting to flip through it*)   All boys his age read this junk. And I think I should probably look inside it, for clues.

Lillian   Where are our letters?

Philip   Hm?

Lillian   Will you put that down! I said: where are our letters?

Mike   Oh, um—yeah, they're not in there.

Lillian   So where does he keep them?

Mike   … That's the thing. He doesn't actually …

Lillian   What … He throws them away?

Philip (*drily*)   Before or after he reads them?

Mike *doesn't say anything.*

Lillian   He doesn't even read them?

Breath.

Mike   I probably shouldn't have—

Philip   It's okay, Lil.

Lillian   It's okay?

Philip   It doesn't mean as much as you think.

Mike   I'm so sorry … I just thought.

Philip (*to* **Mike**)   Don't worry. You didn't do anything wrong.

Mike   I was weighing whether or not to tell you. I didn't wanna upset you.

Lillian   If only our son felt the same way.

Mike   I'm pretty sure he doesn't wanna upset you either.

Philip   Well then he deserves an advanced degree in doing things he doesn't intend to do.

Mike   You're pretty hard on him, aren't you.

Philip . More like not hard enough.

Mike   Sorry. It's not my place.

Philip   No, not really.

Mike *exits.*

Lillian   I mean, why do I do this? Why do I always do this?

Philip   Do what?

Lillian   Even my mother didn't appreciate me. All the time I spent sitting in that awful nursing home.

Philip   Lil—

Lillian   And you! And you, Philip.

Philip   What about me?

Lillian   I don't have the words to …

Philip   In what ways have I failed you, Lillian? In what myriad ways?

Lillian   If you don't know them by now, then we're totally lost.

Philip   Totally lost, huh?

Lillian   Yes.

Philip   We're totally lost?

Lillian   Don't do this.

Philip   What am I doing?

Lillian   So then it's my fault? I see. It's all my fault. My neuroses have made our son neurotic. He's a loner because I was a loner. But so what? I was alone until I met you. And who knows—maybe I will be again.

Philip   What does that mean?

Lillian   But he didn't get his temper from me.

Philip   You wouldn't know it right now, would you?

Lillian   Oh, am I the one who blew up and banished him? No I heard you. You said "get out" to our son. I heard you. As though he were a bug or a dog or a pest. You've really done it this time. You think you can say anything and it won't matter but it does.

Philip   I can't stand this.

Lillian   Tell me, Philip: do you even like him?

Philip   Our kid?

Lillian   That's right.

Philip   Do I like our kid?

Lillian   Right.

Philip   Do *you*??

Beat.

Lillian   I've forgiven you a lot of things, a lot of things, over the years but I won't … I mean, if we don't find him.

Philip   You'll what? What kind of sick threat is this?

Lillian   I don't know!

Philip   In all these years, I have never once threatened I'd walk out the door.

Lillian   I didn't say it.

Philip   You were about to.

Lillian   Well maybe I should! Because if he's dead? I mean, if something's really happened to him?

Philip   Don't say that!!

Lillian   If my son is—

Philip   *Our* son!

Lillian   If he's gone, I'll—

Philip   You'll what? Hole up in yourself? Hide away? Haven't you done that already, Lil? Doesn't that ring a bell?

Lillian   Philip.

Philip   Let me tell you something, Lillian. And you don't want to hear it but you have to. You must. Because it's a fact: we are growing older and we will die.

Lillian   Enough!

Philip   Your mother died and I know you loved her desperately, desperately, that she was your best friend, and that it shocked the fucking bejesus out of you, for her to just not be here anymore. But it happened and it will happen to us and to our children in the blink of an eye—

Lillian   I said: enough!

Philip   No, Lil. Not enough. It's been years now. Years. Life passes by in an instant and that scares the shit out of me too, but our son is who knows where right now and all I can think about is all the time that's been lost, all this time we can't get back when we should have been … I mean, for him if nothing else. God, no wonder he is the way he is! I just can't take it anymore.

Lillian   That's what this is about, Philip. You, not Joseph. You. Your guilt. Your absence.

Philip   No, it's about our family!

Lillian   Which you're well on your way to decimating.

A breath.

Philip (*considered, deadly*)   Lil, you are the love of my life … but maybe you *should* leave.

Lillian looks at him with seething hatred and exits. A long beat. Lights shift and we find **Nora**, *emailing*

Nora   Dear Joey, I don't know where you are or when you'll get this email but I wanted to let you know that there's this song Taylor sings that's about misery. She wrote it a long long time ago, like maybe five years ago, and it goes like this.

She sings a bit of the Taylor Swift song "Fifteen".

   Cause when you're fifteen and somebody tells you they love you
   You're gonna believe them

And when you're fifteen, don't forget to look before you fall
I've found time can heal most anything
And you just might find who you're supposed to be
I didn't know who I was supposed to be
At fifteen

Which is to say that when she wrote this song she had no armor and was just out there almost *asking* to be hurt whereas now in songs like "Shake It Off" she's saying you can't have too many defenses to get through the day. And that's why I find her so brave. Because she isn't afraid to look at the world as it really is.

She exits; **Mike** *enters to listen.*

Lillian   July 7th

Dear Joseph,

I'm so excited to see you in a few days. In fact, I might see you before you even get this letter. So I can tell you now how nice it was to see you. Thank you for a great weekend! I was watching TV just now and there was a sitcom on about a mother and her son and their relationship just seemed too perfect. Too neat. I mean, I know we don't always get along, but it's better that way, isn't it? You know I love you and am always thinking of you and hoping you're okay, and doing your laundry and taking showers. And I'm so excited for lobster! And a cool Maine night. It's been sweltering here. New York in the summer is beastly. You're so smart to get away. And then, to come back. I love you, my sweetheart. Mom.

The lights shift. **Philip** *and* **Lillian** *are on separate parts of the stage, in different places—***Philip** *is in the main lodge and* **Lillian** *is outside, in a field.* **Mike** *enters the lodge.*

Mike   Mr. Nadelman.

Philip   No news?

Mike   No. But I wanted to see if you two needed anything. Is Mrs. Nadelman … ?

Philip   I don't know. I don't know where she is. She went for a walk, I guess.

Mike   Do you need anything? Is there anything I can …

Philip   No.

Beat.

You want a cigarette?

Mike   I used to smoke. Not anymore.

Philip   What—when you were two years old? Your "used to" is my yesterday I think … That's one funny thing about life.

He goes to light a cigarette but then changes his mind.

Oh maybe I shouldn't either. Wooden lodge, right?

Mike   Joey told me he was afraid of fire. When he was a kid.

Philip   Did he?

Mike   Yeah.

Philip   He had a lot of fears, at one point.

Mike   He said he had all these questions and every night you guys would answer them, and make him feel safe.

Philip   He told you about that?

Mike   His long list of fears—

Philip   Do you promise I won't die in my sleep? Do you promise no one will break in? Do you promise I won't wake up in Vermont, on the third grade camping trip? Do you promise you'll still be here in the morning? … And eventually the list got so long that we proposed he just ask: "do you promise all my questions?" Which he did every night before bed, for years. And we'd say yes. And then he could go to sleep.

Mike   Amazing.

Philip   I miss those days. When we could actually …

Mike   … can I ask you something?

Philip   I guess.

Mike   Why do you work so hard?

Philip   What?

Mike   Is it that you prefer being at work?

Philip   Did Joey say that?

Mike   No, I just wondered.

Philip   I don't prefer being at work.

Mike   No?

Beat.

Philip   Which isn't to say it's easy to be home.

A breath.

Mike   I used to have this dream—when I was a kid. I was in the car, with my mom and dad, and suddenly they'd disappear from the front seat and the car would be like driving itself, which was terrifying, and I'd wonder why I hadn't made them stay.

Beat.

Philip   It's rough. Being a kid. You feel so alone. And the shitty thing is, it never goes away.

Mike (*quietly*)   It doesn't?

Philip   Well, yes and no. Maybe you just get used to it. You accept it. And sometimes, if you're lucky, you get distracted from it. Having kids can do that.

Mike   So is that why you work so hard? To distract yourself?

Philip   Why are you asking, Mike?

Mike   I don't know.

Beat.

I guess I have a sort of weird thing with *my* dad.

Philip   So you didn't see him much when you were growing up? Is that it?

Mike   When I was growing up. Does that mean I'm grown up now?

Philip   No.

Mike   … Yeah, I didn't see him much.

A breath.

Philip (*quietly*)   Hey … can I ask *you* something?

Mike   Sure. Of course.

Beat.

Philip   What's he like? ... My son.

Lights shift, to **Lillian**, *on the phone with* **Nora**.

Lillian   Your father is just ... I'm sorry. I know I shouldn't talk about him with you.

Nora   No, it's okay.

Lillian   I'm just not sure that we can ...

Nora   Mom, it's two in the morning and you're under a lot of stress.

Lillian   I don't know.

Nora   You two love each other.

Lillian   Then why is your brother the way he is?

Beat.

Nora   I don't know. But it's not because of you and Dad. I mean, I hear things, like, at school ...

Lillian   What do you hear?

Nora   Like one day he talked to this guy Ethan Carney—

Lillian   Ethan Carney whose mother ran off with Dr. Goldman?

Nora   The orthodontist?

Lillian   Yes!

Nora   The point is: Ethan's, like ... well, he's popular, you know? And I don't think Joey's ever spoken to him before. But I heard he went right up to him and was like "I have Attention Deficit Disorder, ever heard of it?" And Ethan was like "sure, ADD" and then Joey said "but sometimes I actually think I can focus really well, and like, better than other people. What do you think of that, Ethan Carney?"

Lillian   And what did Ethan say?

Nora   I don't think he knew what to say. And then Joey was like "actually I don't have ADD. I have Oppositional Defiant disorder, do you know what that is?" And Ethan said no. And then Joey said, "I don't have that either. I'm actually just depressed. Do you know what that is?" And Ethan said he thought he did; he thought it meant Joey was sad, and then Joey said: "do you like *your* life?" and Ethan, who, for all intents and purposes, has a pretty amazing life, was like "I don't know" and got all thoughtful, at which point Joey just like stood there not saying anything.

I guess I think it was because if Ethan Carney has problems, then where does that leave him.

Lillian   Where does it leave him?

Nora (*getting emotional*)   I don't know, Mom. I don't know where he is.

Lillian   Oh my Nora. What are we going to do?

Beat.

Nora   You remember when Nana asked me at my Bat Mitzvah if I ever prayed and I said not really, that I didn't really believe in God and therefore I didn't believe in prayer.

Lillian   Yes, that caused quite a stir.

Nora   Right. Well. I've been praying tonight. And I think you should too. I think we should do it together.

Lillian   Over the phone?

Nora   Yeah.

Lillian (*to the audience*)   And so we did. And something happened in the silence there, in the tall grass. Into my mind came, for reasons I didn't understand, Philip's subscription to the New York City Ballet when Joseph was young and so needy of me, and what came along with that subscription: his obsession with that dancer Yvonne someone, how he had to see everything she was in: *The Goldberg Variations, Dances at a Gathering, Apollo.* When I went with him I could feel him watching her, following her path around the stage, and then afterwards, I wouldn't—no, couldn't look at him; I felt so abandoned.

And then, one day, the fantasy ended. He canceled his subscription. I asked him why and all he said was that his favorite dancers were getting older, and I nodded and held his hand and understood in that moment that I loved him more than I ever had, maybe, and also that I would never know him.

Nora   So I'm gonna go now.

Lillian   Oh.

Nora   You don't want me to?

Lillian   I don't want you to. I never want you to go.

Nora   Then I won't.

Nora *is crying a little.*

Lillian   Are you okay?

Nora   It's just that sometimes I feel like you don't have time to worry about me. And it's nice to feel worried about. Sometimes.

Lillian   Oh gosh, sweetheart—rest assured I worry about you. My worry knows no bounds. I have enough worry for each of my children and more, I promise you.

Nora   I don't actually want to grow up, Mom. I don't want my life to pass me by.

Lillian   If there's one thing I'm *not* worried about it's your life passing you by.

Nora   You should know: I respect you more than anyone, Mom.

Lillian   That's not true, Nora. But I appreciate it.

Nora   I know you wanted other things for your life.

Lillian   Well, those other things weren't going to be easy.

Nora   You made a choice.

Lillian   And what do I have to show for it?

Nora   Um. What am I? Chopped liver? And Joey?

Lillian   And Joey …

Nora   He's gonna come back, Mom.

Lillian   I hope so, Nora.

Nora   Now will you go find Dad? And sit with him?

The lights shift and **Mike** *is sitting on the dock;* **Joey** *watches him. It's almost daybreak.*

Joey   I just don't get it.

Mike *turns around.*

Mike   Joey!

Joey   I still can't get my mind around … I can't …

Mike   Are you okay?

Joey   I mean, every way I look at it, it's just messed up.

Mike   Do your parents know you're okay?

Joey   I was looking for my sunscreen this morning—my sunscreen, of all things, so I could put some on so when my mom asked me if I was wearing any I could show her and she'd get off my back—and I remembered I leant it to you. So I went through some of your stuff. And behind some of your books, there was a stack of paper.

Mike   Joey—

Joey   And it was my mom's letters …

Mike   Is that what this is all about?

Joey   Why do you have all my mom's letters?

Beat.

Mike   You threw them away.

Joey   That doesn't answer the question. Those were my letters.

Mike   I know. I'm sorry.

Joey   You're sorry? Why'd you want them?

Mike   Why didn't you?

Beat.

Joey   I'm not gonna answer that. I don't have to.

Mike   Fine.

Joey   It's none of your business. And neither were those fucking letters.

Mike   Fine.

Joey   Why do you keep saying "fine"? You're such an asshole.

Mike   I'm an asshole? I'm not the one who took off and left all these people to think I'd killed myself or something.

Joey   Is that what people thought?

Mike   Where'd you go today, Joey?

Joey   Nowhere. I went nowhere. I just sat on a rock and stared at the fucking lake.

Mike   What rock? Where?

Joey At this loon, lifting its head and then lowering it again. All day. This crazy-ass loon.

Mike They were like combing the camp looking for you.

Joey At first you could only just barely see the moon and then it kind of took over the sky.

And all day this fucking song kept going through my head, this song my bunk wrote last summer ... like:

To the tune of "Leaving on a Jet Plane."

>*So hug me and cry with me*
>*Tell me you'll upload your pics*
>*from our summer at Camp Kickapoo*
>*'Cause I'm leaving on a jet plane*
>*I don't know if I'll be back again*
>*oh babe, I hate to go.*

He stops singing.

And it goes on.

Mike You didn't change very many of the lyrics.

Joey Yeah. We didn't win Best Song last year.

And then yesterday, Jimmy Friedlander comes up to me and he's like "is your mom coming for visiting day too?" and I burst out crying. It was the most fucked up thing ever ... I burst out crying. I'm such a freak. I don't understand what's ... I just ... I hate myself, you know that? I wanna die sometimes.

Mike Don't say that.

Joey I mean, how *could* I read my mom's letters?

Mike Well, you pretty much open an envelope, and—

Joey And then all this time just comes pouring out! All this time ...

Mike You're not making any sense.

Joey Like, time my mom spent writing the letter, time she spent worrying, time that hasn't even happened yet—like, all the things she wants to happen but which probably won't ... With me. My life. Her life. Every day I think she's like "that day wasn't good enough and now it's over" and like ... What can I do about that?

Mike (*quietly, gently*)   You can't.

Joey   I mean, *you* wanted to read the fucking letters. Why?

Mike   I don't know.

Beat.

You know how you can tell a lie totally unintentionally, just totally impulsively, and then you have to follow through with it?

Joey   No.

Mike   Okay, the first day, you asked me where my parents lived, just like assuming I had parents and they lived somewhere, and instead of getting into it, I was just like "New Jersey." And then I had parents who lived in New Jersey. I don't know why I said it. And when I saw one of your letters, it seemed like it was from *my* mother … I know it sounds completely crazy …

Beat.

Joey   Why would anyone make up New Jersey? If I were making shit up, it wouldn't be New Jersey.

Mike   Yeah, I don't know.

Beat.

Joey   So you don't have parents.

Mike   My grandma raised me so … right, not really, no …

Beat.

Joey   And you thought *my* parents sounded, like, good?

Mike   Sort of. Yeah. It's complicated.

Joey   It's not. I promise you. There is nothing about my life that anyone has any reason whatsoever to want.

Mike   Are you kidding? I'd kill for someone to write letters like that to me.

Joey   Letters like what?

Mike   Just so filled with empathy, I guess.

Joey   Oh my god. Was all of this just one big acting exercise for you?

Mike   No of course not.

Joey   I think acting is basically just a nice way to say lying by the way. I mean, do you even go to Vassar?

Mike   I go to Vassar.

Joey   ... but you don't have three sisters?

Mike (*a tad bashful*)   No ... It's a play I like, though. I was in it freshman year—

Joey   I told you things I've never told *anyone*.

Mike   I know.

Joey   What else did you make up?

Mike   Nothing else.

Joey   So are we friends? ... Because I haven't ...

Beat.

Because I thought ... Like for the first time I thought.

Long beat.

Why aren't you saying anything?

Beat.

Mike   I don't know, Joey ... I mean, your parents came 500 miles to visit you and you just took off.

Joey   So?

Beat.

Mike   ... So I grew up like right there, like right across the lake.

Joey   What?

Mike (*pointing across the lake*)   That's my grandma's house. That's where I grew up.

Joey   I don't believe you.

Breath.

Mike   And the weird thing is ... I thought I'd never come back to Maine, once I left. And I certainly never thought I'd be here, like this. I mean, I hated these kids. I really hated them. I thought they were all just assholes with trust funds.

Joey They are.

Mike Once when I was like twelve my friends dared me to swim across the lake. I was a good swimmer, or I thought I was, so I was like yeah sure, why not. And I did it. I got all the way to the other side. What I didn't count on was how tired I'd be and how I wasn't gonna be able to get back. So there I was kind of dazed on this beach and suddenly there were these boys all around me. I thought I'd swum myself into Lord of the Flies or something and I was like holy shit is someone gonna bludgeon me with a fucking rock but then I realized where I was. And it was weird cuz I'd never set foot here before. And these boys are just sitting there staring at me with this, like, disdain, and I was just frozen like an idiot. I couldn't say a word. It was like I couldn't get my mouth to work.

Joey Really?

Mike Yeah. And finally this counselor made his way over to me and pulled me up and wrapped a towel around me. He gave me some hot chocolate in the lodge and then ... he drove me home.

Joey And that's why you came back? To get to be a part of this stupid world?

Mike I don't know. Maybe it was to make sure I'd hate it as much as I thought I would. But that's the thing. I've actually kind of ... liked it. Which fucks me up ... It fucks you up too, right?

Joey What does?

Mike When you actually like something ...

Joey No, it doesn't.

Mike No? ... Then you're an even bigger liar than I am, J-Dog.

Lights shift to **Philip** *and* **Lillian**, *sitting apart from each other in the mess hall.*

Lillian The sun was beginning to rise. You could see its fingers stretching across the lake, down the hill.

Philip Lillian and I sat at a distance from each other ... She wouldn't look at me.

(*To* **Lillian**.) I don't think I've been up this late since law school, cramming for exams ...

Beat.

Remember how you'd bring me food? And coffee? In the middle of the night ...

Beat.

That's what you did. And I really loved you for that ... Have I ever thanked you?

Beat.

I was thinking earlier about when Joey was born. The night before Joey was born. Before we had children. Just before our lives changed.

Beat.

You were in labor, but you wouldn't admit it. You were doubled over in agony and you kept saying "I'm not going to have it. I can't" and I said "I think you're gonna have it. One way or another." And you said "Philip, don't make me." You said "I can't have a child; I'm still a child; I can't have a child" and I said I wasn't making you but I'd very much like you to have our child, for us to be a family, finally. We'd waited a long time because we liked our freedom; we were selfish, but then it was almost too late. So we just did it. And then, there you were, in labor, and I was holding you and you told me to let go because if I didn't you worried I'd be holding on forever. But I wouldn't let go. I held on. And you had Joey. And when he was born he had those huge eyes. Like he was so excited to see the world. To try to understand it.

Beat.

Lillian   He did. Enormous eyes.

Philip   And he looked like my father. Which was terrifying. To have my father come out of your body. Coming back to get me. God ... And to think how many times I've wanted to wring that kid's neck.

Lillian (*quietly*)   He's an infuriating kid.

Philip (*with so much love*)   He is an infuriating kid.

Beat.

Please talk to me, Lil.

Lillian   What do you want me to say?

Philip   I don't know.

Beat.

That you love me.

Lillian   You need me to tell you that I love you?

Joey enters. **Philip** *and* **Lillian** *stand up.*

Joey   Mom.

And then in quick succession, or overlapping:

Lillian (*understated—not an outburst*)   Joseph. Oh my god, Joseph.

Philip   Joey. Thank god.

She opens her arms and **Joey** *runs into them, without self-consciousness. The three of them huddle together, as attached as they've ever been; the lines in the next part of the scene overlap and move quickly.*

Joey   I'm ... I'm.

Lillian   Shh ... Shh ...

She rocks him.

You're back. You're safe. That's all that matters.

Joey   Mom.

Lillian   Shh ... My boy. My little boy.

Joey   No—listen to me! I mean ... will you please listen to me?

Lillian   ... yes, of course we will.

Joey   Because I have all these thoughts that I ... All night they were running through my head, and ...

Lillian   And what are those, sweetheart.

Joey   About how you want me to think things matter. That I matter.

Philip   Because you do.

Joey   But maybe I don't. Maybe nothing does and we're all just trying to believe stuff matters to distract ourselves from the fact that we're gonna die.

Lillian   Well, that's a little—

Joey   OR, things do matter. And if that's true I'm *really* fucked—

Lillian   Honey—

Joey   Like, it's awful to think that there might be good things in the world that I just can't ... Like these really nice, good things that I'm never gonna be able to ...

He breaks down in his mom's arms.

Philip   And we didn't take him home because it was the right thing to do—in fact it was probably the wrong thing. We took him home because it was the only thing to do.

Lillian   And the whole drive back to the city—

Philip   We listened to him ... It was the hardest, the toughest, five hours of my life.

Lillian   You want your child to be happy. It's all you want.

Philip   You think you can provide ... happiness and then you realize you can't. It seems so obvious. It seems like we should have known that.

Lights shift.

Lillian   In bed that night, we held each other. Philip and I. Tight.

Philip   And the fact that we made love didn't mean we were happy. More often, people make love for other reasons.

Lillian   But still, it was nice.

(*To* **Philip**.) Do you remember the first time we kissed?

Philip   Do I remember ...

Lillian   Do you?

Philip   Yes.

Lillian   Tell me about it. I want to remember.

Philip   You don't remember?

Lillian   I do. But tell me.

Philip   Well. As I recall ...

Lillian   Yes.

Philip   Weren't we sitting on the couch in your dorm room.

Lillian   Yes.

Philip   We were listening to ...

Lillian   Simon and Garfunkel.

Philip   And it was snowing outside. And the last bus was a few minutes away and I was gonna have to leave.

Lillian   Yes.

Philip   And I said something like "I don't want to go out there, into the snow." And you said you didn't want me to go. And then I knew.

Lillian   Knew what?

Philip   That I could kiss you.

Lillian   And then you did.

Philip   Yes. I did.

Beat.

Lillian   Philip … why does he torture himself the way he does?

Philip   I don't know.

Lillian   Why do I?

Philip *shrugs.*

Will we always?

Philip   I don't know.

Beat.

Kiss me, Lil.

She does.
The lights shift. The family is assembled. **Lillian** *tinkers with the settings on her camera.*

Nora   Okay why is Mom … why is the camera out?

Lillian   I sometimes wonder why I got one of these digital ones. I was just fine before.

Nora   Is this? Are you guys on something?

Philip   We're just gonna take a little picture, okay? So just be … Let's just be … mellow.

Nora   Okay, you're definitely on something.

Joey *(taunting her)*   Nora, why don't you try to be nice for once.

Nora What?

Joey I said, you should like try to be nice to Mom and Dad.

Nora No, I heard what you said, I just—

Lillian Okay, I'm ready! So ... everyone just keep doing what you're doing.

Joey Don't smile?

Lillian You don't have to smile. No one has to smile.

Joey (*genuinely, not snarky*) Then I'm not gonna smile, okay? I just don't feel like smiling.

Lillian That's fine, Joseph.

Philip J-dog.

Joey My name is Joey.

Beat.

Lillian Joey then. Joey. Joey from now on.

Joey (*with exasperated relief*) Thank you, Mom.

Nora (*quietly*) Yes, thank you.

Nora *puts her arm around* **Joey** *and he lets her.*

Philip (*to the audience*) You see, it was quite a weekend. And it would go on the rest of our lives.

Lillian Are you guys ready?

Nora Mom, aren't you going to be in the picture?

Philip Of course she is. That's not up for debate. That was the whole point. The whole family.

Lillian (*to the audience*) But the same thing has different points for different people. And I just look at my family, assembled awkwardly in the morning light, my children still children for a little longer, my beloved son with one sock on and one off, having weathered—no, weathering his life as we all do, and must—and Philip glaring at me, the room filled with Nora's endearing impatience, and I realize I see them; I really see them.

And I wonder: is *this* what I signed up for? Is this what I wanted?

And then—

She looks at them, makes a decision. It's a bittersweet one. The camera clicks.

I take the picture.

Flash.

End of play

The Great Moment

The Great Moment was commissioned, developed, and world premiered in October, 2019 at Seattle Repertory Theatre, Seattle Washington.

Braden Abraham, Acting Artistic Director Jeffery Herrmann, Managing Director

Director: Braden Abraham

Cast

Sarah	**Alexandra Tavares**
Max	**Greg Mullavey**
Jim/Evan	**Eugene Lee**
Susan	**Kathryn Grody**

Stage Manager	Maria Gray
Scenic	Catherine Cornell
Costume	Heidi Zamora
Lighting	Robert Aguilar
Score and Sound	Obadiah Eaves

Opening night October 16, 2019 at Seattle Rep in the Leo K. Theater

Characters

Max—*a boy, a father, a grandfather, a great-grandfather*
Susan—*a girl, a mother, a grandmother*
Jim—*a boy, a father, a grandfather*
Evan—*a boy, still little*
Sarah—*a girl, a mother ... also a playwright*

Evan *and* **Jim** *should be played by the same actor—and, even though* **Evan** *is three/four years old, he should not be played as a child.*

"When I am dead, my dearest"
BY CHRISTINA ROSSETTI

When I am dead, my dearest,
Sing no sad songs for me;
Plant thou no roses at my head,
Nor shady cypress tree:
Be the green grass above me
With showers and dewdrops wet;
And if thou wilt, remember,
And if thou wilt, forget.

I shall not see the shadows,
I shall not feel the rain;
I shall not hear the nightingale
Sing on, as if in pain:
And dreaming through the twilight
That doth not rise nor set,
Haply I may remember,
And haply may forget.

Sarah *walks to the center of the stage, and looks out into the audience.*

Sarah So I was in a Starbucks the other day, trying to write, when I overheard one woman say to another, as they were leaving, "oh my God, thanks so much for making the time," to which the other replied, "No, thank *you* for making the time."

Which is kind of funny … Right? This idea of "making time"—as though the time that already exists *isn't* finite—it can be added to, if we can only figure out how.

It suggests we actually have some power over time, doesn't it?

That we can, in some sense, create it.

Jim/Evan *barges in.*

Jim/Evan (*playing both of them*) I have questions.

Sarah Oh—this is my father. And also my son. It's a little confusing but I think you'll get used to it.

Evan I *said*: I have questions.

Sarah Right now he's my son, Evan. He's three … And also Four. And five …

Evan Why don't you ever listen to me, Mom?

Sarah He's growing but right now he's still small. Some things he regularly asks include:

Evan Is Great-grandpa dead yet?

When will he die?

What happens if a kid is hit by a car?

Can a kid die?

How does it feel to die?

When will Grandma and Grandpa die?

Were you the first person?

What happens when forever ends?

Will you be alive when I'm a grownup?

Will you let me know when I'm an old man?

Will you let me know when I'm about to die?

What time will it be tomorrow?

Sarah   He asks this last question—what time will it be tomorrow—
every night right before he falls asleep. Invariably one of us is lying
next to him—(*conspiratorial with the audience*) because he has us
wrapped around his finger—and we know when we hear this question
that, finally, sleep is close. My husband responds that it will be tomorrow
one minute—one second—after midnight. My interpretation is different.
I say that *every* time on the clock will happen tomorrow; tomorrow holds
all of time.

Our gaze shifts to an old man, **Max,** *trying and failing to get out of a chair.*

Max   Getting old sucks.

Sarah   This is my grandfather. He's ninety-eight years old. And:

Max   Getting old sucks

Sarah   Is something he says to me
and that I write down
in the hope of saving his voice after he's gone.

He says, "Sarah, let me tell you something. Getting old sucks" every
time I see him.
And right now, during the holidays, he's staying with my parents, as
are we,
so I see him all the time.

Right now, when I write these words, it is December 23rd, two thousand
and sixteen.
But when, or if, you hear them it will inevitably be later.

This is a moment in time.

I am thirty-seven.

It's the age my mother was when I first became aware she had an age.
And when you first become aware of your mother's age, that age seems
very old.
My friends and I joke that one day thirty-seven will seem young so
there's no sense in feeling down about it.

But today my grandfather says:

Max   Sarah, you're getting old too, I guess.

Sarah   But don't I seem young to *you*?

Max   No, not really.

Sarah   Four months ago, I was thirty-six. And a week past my due date. I was sitting on the couch watching this movie based on the true story of this guy Ramanujan who's so good at math he gets a fellowship to Cambridge or Oxford or one of those places in like 1914. From India. And the movie is so heartwarming, about Ramanujan succeeding against all odds—against poverty, against racism—that when he drops dead at the age of thirty-two, it is really actually very shocking and sad because it seemed like it was going to be a different story.

Jim   Max, would you like a cup of coffee?

Sarah   (*You see, now he's my Dad. You get it.*)

Jim   Max? Would you like a cup of coffee?

Max   What was that?

Jim (*much louder*)   Coffee??

Max   Oh thanks, Jim, I'd love that yes.

Sarah   And while I'm watching the movie, unbeknownst to me, my body is deciding that it's time for my little boy, my second child, to come live in the world. For hours I don't think this is what's happening, even though all I've been doing for weeks now is waiting. I don't think this is what's happening even in the taxi with my husband and my mother that evening. "Let's not go straight to the hospital," I say.

Then, realizing.

Maybe all of this is an attempt to stave off the forward march of time.

And when he's born I look at my son, and I see my grandfather ... and I think: let him live. Let him live and live and live and live.

Jim   Didn't I offer you coffee a few minutes ago? I think I offered it to you and then forgot to make the cup.

Max   I only got three of those words.

Jim (*really really loud*)   I said—did I offer you coffee and then forget to make the cup?

Max   Oh! Yes. But you know what? I don't want it anymore.

When all is said and done, Jim, growing older sucks.

And you know one of the more objectionable things also really that you can't control is—to phrase it delicately … a thing known as leakage.

But when all is said and done there are compensations. And the kids, no doubt, are compensations for what goes on.

Jim   Your grandchildren are incredibly cute.

Sarah   He means great-grandchildren. But my father can't wrap his head around being a grandfather. At least not in the presence of my grandfather who seems to own the name he's had so long.

Jim   I took a very nice picture of you and Evan.

Max   What?

Jim   I said, I took a very nice picture of you and Evan!

Max (*not hearing him*)   Okay.

Jim *shows* **Max** *the photo on his phone.*

Max   Who is that—Evan?

Jim   This is the picture I was just telling you about.

Max   Yes, Jim, there's no doubt, it's one of the blessings that exists in life, no doubt about it …

Jim   We're very lucky.

Max   There used to be a *marvelous* song by Eddie Fisher "Count your Blessings." I doubt you'd remember it.

Sarah (*to the audience, raising an eyebrow*)   So this is why Evan now uses the word marvelous.

Jim   Let's see if we can find it.

Doing a search on his phone.

It looks like Bing Crosby sang it.

Max   You're going to prove me wrong.

Jim   Just because Spotify doesn't have Eddie Fisher doesn't mean Eddie Fisher didn't do it.

Max   It's the thing I remember most about Eddie Fisher: (*Sings*) "Oh my papa … to me you are so wonderful …"

Sarah   This is the song my mother sings to the baby when she's rocking him to sleep. Only she changes the lyrics:

We hear **Susan** *singing offstage:*

Susan   *Oh Benjamin, to me you are so wonderful,*
Oh Benjamin, to me you are so good.

Sarah   I had no idea this was a song her father sang when she was a child. I thought she made it up.

Jim   Let's try a different … Hold on … Apple music. Search: Count … Your … Blessings.

Max   Aren't these things miracles.

Jim   Well except I'm still not …

Sarah   Try searching a different title, maybe.

Jim   Oh! … Yes—good. There it is: "Oh My Papa".

It's been recorded by *a lot* of people. Diana Krall. Rosemary Clooney. Barbara Cooke. The Mormon Tabernacle Choir! … and … wait for it— Eddie Fisher! I had to scroll all the way down.

Max   You mean I was right?

Jim   You were right!

The song plays—loud. After they listen for a bit, **Max** *interrupts.*

Max   Isn't that amazing?

I remember once saying to you "it was a very good year" and instantaneously I had Frankie.

Susan (*entering*)   Isn't that a little loud? Won't it wake up the boys?

Sarah   They're fine, Mom.

Susan   It's just that Evan so needs his sleep. Otherwise he's a crazy man the next day and I don't particularly want him drawing on my walls again.

Sarah   Or maybe that was because you let him eat cookies for lunch.

Susan   Well, he *likes* cookies.

Sarah   Of course he does.

Susan   He doesn't exactly have a varied palate, Sarah.

Sarah   He's also three years old.

Susan (*lightly*)   I suppose I think that if you made a concerted effort, you could start to incorporate more foods into his diet. But maybe you just don't have the time?

Sarah (*turning to* **Jim**/*changing the subject*)   Eddie Fisher was Carrie Fisher's father, right?

Jim   I'm surprised you know who Eddie Fisher is.

Sarah   And I think he was Jewish.

Susan   No, I very much doubt that. Eddie Fisher?

They all search on their phones.

Jim   He was. And Russian. One of seven children. And married *five* times!

Susan   Well that's … energetic.

Max   I seem to recall he left Debbie Reynolds for Elizabeth Taylor. Which means he was lucky.

Jim   Why's that?

Max   If Elizabeth Taylor had met me first, he'd have been toast.

Sarah   And then a nonsequitur. It's often like my grandfather is having a conversation in his head that he continues out loud. He can't distinguish between one world and the other. My mother says this is called withdrawing. That he is starting to withdraw.

Max   Talk about irony. When I saw *Sweeney Todd* on Broadway some of the scenery fell down on stage in the middle of Angela Lansbury's number:
"Nothing's gonna harm you
Not while I'm around
Nothing's gonna harm you
No sir, not while I'm around"

He makes the sound of the scenery crashing.

It was, in its way, perfect.

Beat.

Sarah   The other night he said to me:

Max (*realizing*)   You know, the thing about being this age is: everyone I know is dead.

Sarah   Well, not everyone.

Max   And everything is behind you. You spend all this time being nostalgic. You spend so much time just thinking.

Sarah   Too much thinking?

Beat.

Max (*sadly/reflectively*)   Yes.

Sarah   Does he wonder every night if he'll wake up again?

Max (*reflective*)   "All, all are sleeping. Sleeping on the hill."

Do you know what that is?

Sarah   I don't.

Max   Really, Sarah, you surprise me. It's from *Spoon River Anthology*.

Sarah   Those are poems?

Max   What?

Sarah   Poems?

Max (*reflective*)   I happen to think they were very good people. Grandma, Joseph, Edna, my parents … I really do think they were good people.

Evan   Mom, let's architect something.

Sarah (*to* **Max**)   Is it less daunting, thinking about … knowing that all of them have done it already? … Gone before you?

Evan   Did you hear me, Mom?

Sarah (*looking down, a bit ashamed*)   I wish I had the courage to ask that.

Max   All, all sleeping on the hill.

Evan   Mom!!

Sarah   What?

Evan   I'm talking to you. I want to architect something.

Sarah   Like build something?

Evan   Yes.

Sarah   What do you want to build?

Evan   A new Brooklyn.

Sarah   What, you don't like the old Brooklyn anymore?

Evan   Next to our house in New Brooklyn will be waiting rooms. And hotels. Which will have lanterns. You have to write that down. About the lanterns. Did you write that down, Mom?

Sarah   Oh you want me to write this down?

Evan   Yes! All of what I say.

Sarah   Okay.

Evan   Write our names okay, Mom?

Sarah   Whose names?

Evan   My name is Rah. Benjamin's name is Dead.

Sarah   Excuse me?

Evan   Benjamin is Dead. In New Brooklyn, my little brother Benjamin is Dead and I am Rah.

Sarah   Like the Egyptian sun god?

Evan   What's a god?

Sarah (*brightly, trying to get out of this*)   Oh. Um. Yeah. I don't, um—

Evan (*interrupting*)   And I will architect fireplaces and a bullet train and a regular bus and also a double decker bus. And Benjamin will go on it and never come back.

Sarah   Evan, are you feeling angry about your brother being here?

(*turning to the audience.*) This is what we've been told we should ask. We've also been told to say we miss the time when it was just the three of us. That this should make him quicker to accept his brother.

Evan (*totally matter-of-fact*)   Yes, I hate him. When will he die?

Susan *is on the phone.*

Susan   No, I don't like you to have to do that. We could get a nurse … Is that what he says? He really won't even consider it? If only assisted living could assist those who are too stubborn to get assistance, right?

I mean, it's no wonder he couldn't hold down a job. He won't do anything anyone tells him to—still! At ninety-eight years old. Everything else goes, but not that.

Sarah   Mom ...

And then **Susan** *is off the phone.*

Susan   It's almost impressive. If it weren't so infuriating.

Sarah   What's going on?

Susan   Well, I guess he's gotten worse. Vicky says he's gotten worse.

Sarah   Worse how?

Susan   Oh I don't know, Sarah. Worse. You know, falling down, things like that.

Sarah   Falling down??

Susan   And of course he won't accept help. He won't even get his hearing aids tuned up. This is what he's always been like. Everything done his way, on his terms. It drove my mother crazy.

Sarah   It doesn't really matter, though, does it? We just have to keep him safe.

Susan   I know. I said: get an aide. I mean, he has the money. He can pay for it. You know there's no love lost between me and my sister but it's just not fair to her, to Vicky. I can't stand that she has to keep checking on him to make sure he's not dead.

Sarah   I think that's better than the alternative.

Susan   She says it would be a good thing, for him to die in his sleep. Isn't that what any of us really wants? Just to die in our sleep?

Sarah (*quietly*)   Is it?

Beat.

Susan (*sadly*)   But then he'd be gone.

Sarah (*to the audience*)   My grandma Rose died ten years ago, but was really gone ten years before that. During that period my grandfather never left her side, even after she stopped remembering him, after she stopped remembering herself. So he arguably spent his last good years in this purgatory of ... But I'm not sure it felt that way to him. To him, she was—

Max   Everything. My sunshine.

Sarah (*finishing his sentence*)   "Grandma Sunshine" is what we all called her. Really. And in my memory she *was* very sunny, always laughing and doling out tic-tacs. But today my mother said:

Susan   Sunny? No. She was depressed. Angry. My whole childhood, really.

Sarah   She was?

Susan   She'd have these episodes where she wouldn't get out of bed. For weeks sometimes.

Sarah   What? Why didn't you ever tell me that?

Susan   Didn't I tell you?

Sarah   No.

Susan   I'm sure I told you at some point.

Sarah   I'm pretty sure I'd remember that. That grandma was seriously depressed.

Susan   Oh, well. Maybe. But memory is a funny thing.

Sarah   So it was really bad?

Susan   I don't know. It was just … life, I guess. But I think, for Dad, she was never anything less than perfect.

Sarah   That just … it explains so much.

Susan   About my father.

Sarah   No, about me, I want to say. Or you. Or sadness that sometimes feels like it pervades everything.

Susan   I think she felt cheated out of … I mean, as you know she wanted to be an actress and did a little bit of that when she was young, but then it just kind of dropped away and my guess is she probably felt quite purposeless for most of her life.

Sarah   God, Mom.

Susan   I think all it explains about me is why I made sure I was on a path. A sort of safe path. Not that I was ever cut out to be any sort of artist. Which is why it was so hard for me at first that you … I just didn't ever want you to feel you'd failed.

Sarah *stares at* **Susan**, *not sure what to say, and then turns to the audience.*

Sarah   My grandma Rose was buried in an enormous cemetery in Valhalla, New York on an icy January morning. They had been living in Florida the past couple decades and I couldn't help thinking we were adding insult to injury by burying her in such cold ground.

Max   I remember going back years ago in Camp Swego we had a play, and one of the songs in the play was "All the World's Just a Little Clock Shop". Tick tock.

It's funny how those things stay in your mind.

God knows why.

Sarah   We're sitting together after the boys have gone to sleep. I'm taking notes while he talks, but I don't think he notices.

Max   Maybe it's things you enjoyed. The things you enjoyed stay in your mind better. And the things that have caused you pain don't stay in your mind that much, I don't think.

Sarah   Really? Because I could recite for you word for word every bad review I've ever gotten.

Max   You know, I once got a quarterly job review, just a kind of, just a routine thing, and on the sheet of paper they handed me it said one word; do you wanna know what it was? Fired.

Sarah   Which job was that?

Max   What's that, Sarah?

Sarah   Which job was that??

Max   Oh who knows. And it doesn't matter. It couldn't matter less … You know what matters? Your backhand. And how's the old—

He makes a tennis serving motion.

Sarah   I don't really get to play very much anymore.

Max   What was that?

Sarah   I don't play anymore. I can't fit it in.

Max   What did you say—you don't play?

She nods.

What, too busy?

She nods.

It's a demanding time of life, I imagine. And, you know, I'm in much the same boat. My schedule just doesn't allow me to fit in the tennis anymore. If only my life were a little emptier, you know? (*He smiles*) No but really Sarah I do happen to think it's one of the great pleasures that exists. Hitting a ball like that.

Sarah   It hangs in the air, unspoken. He has hit his last tennis ball.

Max   Now Sarah look up for me if you will: "The Big Moment." It's a movie. And if I'm not mistaken the leading man was a fellow by the name of Joel McCrea.

Sarah   I google frantically. "Joel McCrea filmography."

The *Great* Moment, I say. Do you mean *The Great Moment?*

He puts his finger on his nose.

Max   Bingo.

What year was that film made?

Sarah   It says 1944.

Max   The movie had to do with the beginning of anesthesia. The invention of anesthesia. I mean, can you imagine the unbelievable pain of extreme surgery without anesthesia? Just a bit of wood to bite on. And then here comes this fellow, Morton, and he invents laughing gas. Hallelujah. He saves millions of people untold pain. Numbs the pain of the world. And still, he's forgotten.

How's that for gratitude.

Sarah   And that's what the movie's about?

Max   What?

Sarah   *The Great Moment.*

Max   What??

Sarah   That's what the movie's about? This guy who was forgotten? Wait, what was his name again?

He can't hear her joke.

Max .   What did you say?

Sarah I said—

Max It's okay. Don't struggle.

Sarah (*as in, it's not a struggle*) Grandpa—

Max It was a good movie as I recall. And that Joel McCrea was an excellent leading man. Even if he was forgotten he got his moment, right?

Sarah (*to the audience*) Later that night I hear him creaking his way to the bathroom downstairs. And I hear my baby waking upstairs, the floor creaking with my husband's weight as he sways him back to sleep, my parents snoring in the other room.

The Great Moment, I think.
The Great Moment.

Susan *enters.*

Susan So have you figured out yet when you're going to be away?

Sarah I'm a playwright. If that isn't clear because, well, this is a play. And one thing about being a playwright is you are often going away.

And a sidebar: I'm not a playwright because my grandfather loved musicals and would play them all the time on the piano when I was a girl. He would sing songs from *The Fantasticks* and *Oklahoma*, from *South Pacific* and *Carousel*, badly and at the top of his lungs, until my grandmother would scream from the other room:

"That's enough, Max. That's enough."

I am not a playwright for that reason except also maybe I am.

Susan When will you be away in June for instance?

Sarah I'm not sure yet. I can't focus on it right now.

Susan Well I have to try to clear my schedule a little for when you're gone. If you want my help.

Sarah I want your help.

Susan And of course we don't know what Grandpa's status will be.

Sarah No, we don't.

Susan Well.
There's a lot of uncertainty these days.
All around.

Sarah   This is a statement my mother could make truthfully any day of her life. Things she's been anxious about include but are certainly not limited to:

Susan   Department stores; suspicious-looking moles; driving at night; slipping on ice; being alone in the house; my children losing their jobs, or really anything that could happen to my children, and trust me I've thought of every possibility, however remote. Let's see, what else … Toxic gas in the New York City subway system; my grandchildren choking on food their parents haven't cut into small enough bites; small spaces and also … big spaces; the undoubtedly deleterious effects of Diet Coke or specifically Nutrasweet, especially in relation to yet-to-be conceived grandchildren; the physical and verbal development of grandchildren already born; the fear they won't be athletic enough, because you see they're all boys. Everything about airplanes.

So, you know, I think Evan senses it. The uncertainty. He's so anxious. I suppose he comes by it honestly. You were such a fearful child, after all.

Sarah   I wonder why.

Susan   What was that?

Sarah   Also, we do cut their food into small enough bites. And we took that CPR course.

Susan   But do you remember any of it? You can't take a course *once* and think that you …

I just think you have to be very careful.
Precious cargo, right?

Sarah   When we were kids, this is what my grandfather would say before we set off on any trip, even if it was just to the deli, or the supermarket. He'd turn around from the driver's seat, survey me and my brothers, and say "is everyone strapped? I've got precious cargo here." Precious cargo.

Susan   So most of June then? Can't you break it into a couple shorter trips? I think that would be so much better for the boys.

Sarah   But I don't have control over it, Mom.

Susan   Why not? It's your play, isn't it?

Sarah   Can you just not …

Susan   What? I didn't say anything.

Sarah   I wait.

Susan (*not able to help herself*)   … it's only that I think it's so hard on Evan. When you're away. When I was your age I made sure to be home for dinner every night. When we wanted to see friends, we had them over. Or we'd go to their houses, with you guys. Order a pizza. We didn't really leave you.

Sarah   And was that fun?

Susan   Fun. Who said anything about fun?

Sarah   Evan is starting to understand that I write plays. I think mostly he thinks that this means I create over and over again EXACTLY the one play he's seen, based on a popular series of books, in which an elephant and a pig who are friends but whose friendship is understandably fraught because the elephant is sweet but dim-witted and the pig is clever and sometimes cruel come on and off the stage singing and being frustrated with each other and then reconciling. "I liked the trumpet," Evan reported afterwards, one detail selected from an hour of details.

Evan   What's that?

Sarah   Evan's looking at a poster on the wall in our kitchen. It's been there all his life but for some reason, at three and a half, he takes it in. I explain it's a poster for a play I wrote a while ago called *The Minotaur*.

Evan   What's a minotaur?

Sarah   Well, it's a creature from Greek myth.

Evan   I don't know any of those words.

Sarah   Right.

Okay, well … in this case a creature is a sort of imaginary being. It's not a person but also not an animal. In the case of the minotaur, it's a half man, half bull.

Evan   Is it real?

Sarah   No. It's part of a myth. And myths are stories we tell. Stories that have been passed down for centuries.

Evan   Why would people tell stories about something that isn't real?

Sarah   Well, most stories are made up. And we make up stories to …
help us understand our lives and what we're doing here. And to provide
us with comfort and the feeling of being less alone.

Evan (*unsatisfied*)   … Why would someone feel all alone?

Sarah   Oh. I think, um … there are some … things in life that can make
us … feel lonely, sometimes even when we're with other people.

Evan   What things.

Sarah   Well.

Evan   Sad things?

Sarah   Yeah.

Sad things.

Evan   And is the Minotaur sad?

Sarah   Sometimes he is. Just like anyone.

Evan   Which part of the play is the Minotaur in?

Sarah   Oh. The whole thing.

Evan (*incredulous*)   The whole thing??

Sarah   Well, not the very end. He's not in the very end. But he's in the
rest of the play.

Evan (*taking this in, not sure he's happy about it*)   Okay.

Sarah   I'm relieved that he doesn't ask why he's not in the end of the
play, which is of course because he dies.

Evan   Why isn't he in the end of the play? Is it because he dies?

Sarah   I can't conjure the person who wrote that play. I was in my 20s
and I think pretty consumed by other people's success. Or depressed.
Probably I was depressed. But I believed things would change,
eventually. Which a decade on, they have—in some ways. For one,
I met John, at a friend of a friend's birthday party neither of us was
really invited to; I almost didn't go: I was wearing a dress and a friend's
beat-up sneakers because my shoes had been giving me blisters; I looked
ridiculous.

Evan   I think we should write a play together, Mom.

Sarah   But John sat across from me and we began a conversation that's still underway. He couldn't have cared less about my shoes. We had two children. Things changed ... And yet in other ways, it feels as though nothing has changed at all.

Evan   Mom! Did you hear me? I said—

Sarah   Okay what should happen in the play we write together?

Evan   I think ... if you bring a toy then the other person should say thank you.

Sarah   So you're saying there could be two characters and one brings the other a toy? And the one who gets the toy should say thank you?

Evan   No, that's not what I said!

What I said is what if you bring a toy and what if they want to keep it and you give it to them and and and you say thank you—THAT'S what I said. That's the first part of the play. So do what I said for the play. Okay, Mom? Okay?? Okay?

Sarah   Okay.

Evan   That is a really good idea, Mom. That is. It is.
There's something else I want to tell you too.
There has to be another Minotaur play.

Sarah   Another one? Why?

Evan   So he can be in the end of the play this time. If I turn into the Mom when I'm grown up then I'LL write a play of Minotaur. And he should say, when it's the end, he should say to elephant and piggy—

Sarah   Oh elephant and piggy are in the play with the Minotaur?

Evan   YES Mom. And at the end, when when when minotaur's on the stage, he says thank you to *you*: thank you for writing me in your play.

Sarah   Wow that's nice of him. I wish all my characters thanked me for writing them into my plays.

Evan   And what comes on the stage at the very very very end is ... US. At the very very very end, we come on the stage—you and me. Together.

Sarah   Do we sing a little song?

Evan   We do.
And then we get off the stage and that's the end of the play.

Sarah (*echoing*)   And that's the end of the play.

Susan   So Vicky called last night. She's saying things aren't good. That he just seems so frail all of a sudden.

Sarah   Like he's …

Susan   I don't know, Sarah.

Sarah   Okay. Okay, so we'll go down.

Susan   Good. Yes. Today?

Sarah   It's a Wednesday morning. I arrange for a series of last-minute babysitters and then—

Evan   No. Please don't leave me, Mom.

Sarah   Evan don't say that.

Evan   I'm sorry that I said it, Mom, it's just that I meant it.

Sarah   And then I leave. I leave the boys and I go with my mother down to Washington DC. This is February 2017. A moment in time. We sit around the kitchen table in my aunt's house, and the morning feels … translucent, as though you can see something on the other side of it.

I'm taking notes, as usual. Inside and outside the moment at the same time. I've always been like this. In First Grade I was probably nostalgic for kindergarten. It just felt so unbearably sad to me, to have to get older. Even when I was a child.

Max   When I was a waiter, *I* always made sure to put all the utensils down on the table.

Sarah (*to the audience*)   My grandfather is teasing Wanda, the woman hired to help him, because she gave him eggs and forgot to bring a fork.

Max   This was at Scaroon Manor.

Susan   I thought it was Schroon Lake?

Max   Yes it was.

Susan   But you said Scaroon Manor.

Max   Yes.

Susan   So was it Scaroon Manor or Schroon Lake??

Max   Both! It was Scaroon Manor on Schroon Lake. I was a waiter and all the women would pinch my cheek when I gave them their food.

This was during college. Very frankly it was a hard job. No time off and then when you were through with your job and you were all clean and polished you had to go out in the evening and dance with the females.

Susan   Like a *Dirty Dancing*-type experience. When I saw that movie I thought of you at Schroon Lake.

Max   You know you're testing my memory. This is going back a few years but there was one entertainer that had the same name as Grandma's friend Ruth Desmond and she loved to dedicate songs to me.

Susan   You were a real heartthrob.

Max   I was a what?

Susan   A heartthrob. A studly guy.

Sarah   Please never say that again Mom.

Max   Well I was uncommonly handsome.

Sarah   I wait for a disclaimer, but … no.

Max   Rose always used to say about me: a flock of sheep and he the only ram, no wonder he's the wonder of Siam.

Susan   Probably because you had the same kind of temper as the king in the *King and I*.

Max   When we were in Denver Vicky played one of the children in the "Dance of the Chinese Children".

Sarah (*to the audience*)   This is horrifying for many reasons of course.

Max   Do you remember that, Susie?

Susan   Yes, because it was me. Not Vicky.

Max   Vicky was such a good little dancer. Do you remember?

He hums the tune to the "March of the Siamese Children".

And that strange little getup they had her in.

Susan   Okay. Dad.

Max   At Schroon Lake Ruth Desmond would sing me this song, something about "my man—an ordinary guy … he's just my boy, an ordinary guy."

Sarah (*to the audience*)   I look it up and it's Bill, from *Showboat*.

Susan   Sarah says it's Bill from *Showboat!*

Sarah   But that must not have been one of your favorites. You didn't play *Showboat* for us. It was mostly *Oklahoma. Carousel. Camelot.*

Max   What was that?

Susan   *Oklahoma! Carousel! Camelot!*

Max   "C'est moi, C'est moi." Oh how I do love that noble Sir Lancelot. Except I think he gets involved with Queen Guinevere so maybe actually he's not so noble.

Sarah (*to the audience*)   And then we are talking about money, which often comes up because it's a topic of great interest to my grandfather. For so many years he had no money, or very little, in part because he had trouble holding down a job in part because he never found a job that made him happy, which might be another way of saying he had some trouble with authority.

Susan   So did you buy anything last night or were you just thinking?

Sarah (*to the audience*)   He was a basketball player. A star in the thirtiess. We have a book of clippings and he peers out from its pages, looking slim and serious in black and white. He spent the war playing basketball in Alaska, entertaining troops. But when he went pro, he got injured quickly and his career ended, at which point he became an accountant because he had to do something.

Max   Susie, I don't buy, I sell.

Sarah (*to the audience*)   We always say he should have been an English teacher since he loves books and knows so many poems by heart—an idea we toss off casually, but describes the *entirety* of his life.

Susan   More puts?

Max   No. No more than I had. But I was thinking today if I sell more puts I'll get rid of my debt.

Sarah (*to the audience*)   But after he retired he started playing the market, and that did go pretty well, and now, suddenly, he's interested in money. Maybe you can only be interested in money once you have some.

Susan   Your margin you mean?

Max   Well, it's like a margin, yes.

Susan   Well, the only problem is you're betting hard the market's not gonna crash; you're very exposed.

Max   Betting hard that it won't crash as low as the point that I'm vulnerable. And the market's up today. Who knows why.

Susan   You're all puts; you don't have any calls out.

Sarah (*to the audience*)   I don't have any idea what any of this means.

Susan   And the danger is that we do have a crazy person running the country.

Max   Well, you know what they say: no risk no reward.

Sarah   Mom would pick no reward in that equation.

Susan   You're right; I would.

Max   Susan I'm very much like Tony Soprano. So he killed people. The question is when to jump out. When to take what you have and run.

Sarah   And I think: a) my grandfather watched *The Sopranos*? And b) … he's talking about dying … This is the way he is going to talk about dying.

Susan   You probably want to hold onto your dividend stocks—to provide you with income.

Sarah   What she doesn't articulate is the question of how long he'll need income, but it's there. Which might be why he changes the subject.

Max   I was telling Wanda the other day that I'd never seen a *Star Wars* movie, if you can believe it. And then I watched that one with you all and I'll be honest with you—maybe it's my condition but I wasn't overwhelmed by it.
It wasn't nearly as good as that movie I loved with the girl going to the dance contest.

Sarah   You're comparing *Star Wars* to *Little Miss Sunshine*?

Max   *Little Miss Sunshine*. Yes!

Oh I thought that was a very funny and good movie.
And the way they got rid of the grandpa, played by that young fella Alan Arkin.

Susan   Dad, Alan Arkin is in his eighties now!

Max   Another movie that I enjoyed was called *The Fighter*. You know why I'm thinking of *The Fighter*, don't you?

Sarah   He smiles and points to his arm, which is black and blue from falling yesterday.

Max   Oh Sarah, getting old sucks … But I must say I really did get a kick out of that physical therapist who came over yesterday. She had me test sitting on the toilet. I wanted to say, you know I've done this a few times.

Susan   Are you tired, Dad?

Max   Yes I think I'll take my morning hiatus now.

Sarah   How long does it last?

Max   I don't have control of it.
But I do like my word hiatus. I think that's appropriate.
If you're, shall we say, "mature," like I am, it's easier to get tired.

Sarah   I think of how badly we always want Benjamin to go to sleep. How that's the deal with babies. But with the old, well we want the old to stay awake.

Max   My phrase is: it goes with the territory. "Grow old along with me, the best is yet to be." *Rabbi Ben Ezra*. By Robert Browning I'm going to guess.

Sarah   I look it up and he's right. Robert Browning.

Max   And by the way that is such a lie: "The best is yet to be."

In fact I used to have my own private joke really. That I'd go to the burial site of Browning and show him what I thought of this misguided thing he'd written.

Sarah   Whenever I say goodbye to my grandfather I don't know if I'll see him again.
Still, you have to be casual about it, right?
You just have to kiss him on the cheek. Make a joke.
… You never know when you've done something for the last time …

Evan   I won't do it.

Sarah   Back at home, Evan has been resisting doing something for the *first* time. Using the potty.

Evan   Nope.

Sarah   Sometimes I think he's afraid to try for fear of failing.
Sometimes I think he doesn't want to grow up. Maybe because he says:

Evan   I want to be a baby like Benjamin. How about we make him the big boy and me the baby.

Sarah   He's always making excuses. Tonight he's sitting in the middle of the living-room, naked and passing gas. He says, without prompting:

Evan   No, Mom. There's no pee behind that fart.
And no poo behind that fart.

Sarah   And then, as though to distract me from the task at hand:

Evan   So what did Grandma look like in olden times?

Sarah   Is it possible that I say "olden times"??

Evan (*getting impatient*)   Mom?!

Sarah   She looked young, Evan. I mean, once, she was my age. Once, if you can believe it, she was even your age. She was three.

Evan   Where was I when grandma was three?

Sarah   … The radiator creaks and then moans. I look around the room. At the walls and the ceiling and the floor and the windows and the trees outside the windows and the darkness beyond the trees. Where was Evan when his grandmother was three. I say:

Well, you didn't exist yet.

Evan   What does that mean?
Where was I before I was born?

Sarah   The other morning I was in bed with Benjamin, drifting in and out of sleep. It was early, five, maybe six. In what must have been a dream but at the time seemed so real my father walked into the room. He looked the way he did when I was born. Thirty. Thirty-one. The way he looked when we were on Shelter Island my first summer and I was in one of those seats in the back of his bicycle wearing a little bonnet. He even had on the glasses he wore then. He was holding a stack of photographs and putting them into some kind of container on the bedside table. He smiled sadly at me, as though to acknowledge that none of this made sense but also here we were. The envelope of time folding in on itself. Here we are in the mystery of it all.

Evan   Oops. Pee came out. And poop came out.
I'm sorry, Mom.

Sarah   For awhile after Evan was born I kept a diary. First I wrote in it every day, recording as much as I could, each little sound, the tilt of his head as he slept. Before long, I was writing in it every few days, then once a month. Now it's been years since I wrote in that little diary.

Why did I think it was okay to stop?

Jim   Oh my god, Sarah.

Sarah   Later that day I saw my father. He'd just had *gum* surgery and was in a terrible mood.

Jim (*through clenched teeth; we can barely understand him*)   They ran out of general anesthetic.

Sarah   What do you mean they ran out?

Jim   They ran out. And he said "would you do it with the local?" He said most people do it with the local. And, you know, I wanted to get it over and done with. But actually I wish I'd waited.

Sarah   It was that bad?

Jim   First of all, your mouth keeps filling with blood—

Sarah (*I've heard enough*)   Okay.

Jim   And you can feel him sort of peeling the gum back, lifting the gum away from the teeth—

Sarah   Dad, that's—

Jim   I could feel it the whole time. *Two hours.*

Sarah   Two hours?

Jim   And now I'm on a liquid diet.

Sarah   For how long.

Jim   A month maybe.

Sarah   Holy shit.

Jim   I know.

Sarah   I've never even heard of gum surgery before.

Jim   Because you're not sixty-eight years old.

Sarah   I have the cholesterol level of a sixty-eight year old. Thanks for that by the way.

(*To the audience.*)

Also people my age are starting to die. Three women I know from college have cancer. My husband's high school classmate died last year and everyone in their class went to his funeral, not boys anymore. But still, if we are relatively healthy, we blithely assume we will continue to live. That we are saved, somehow. Is there any way around that feeling?

Jim   Did you get a new cholesterol test?

Sarah   Yeah. It's high.

Jim   Okay, and …

Sarah   And he wants me to go on a higher dose of Lipitor.

Jim   Well but didn't he expect it would go up? I mean, did he say your cholesterol was higher than it should be, given you were off the meds when you were pregnant?

Sarah   I'm not sure.

Jim   Well maybe you have to call back and ask.

Sarah   Yeah, maybe I will.

Jim   You probably won't.

Sarah   I probably won't.

Max   Sarah—

Sarah   Back in Washington, my grandfather wakes up from his nap, a little dazed the way Benjamin is when he wakes up.

Max   Sarah—

He points across the room.

Sarah   What … you want water?

He points again.

Something from the fridge?

He puts his finger on his nose.

Orange juice?

He keeps his finger there. She brings the juice.

Max   Thank you awfully Sarah.

Sarah   How was your nap?

Max   Oh I stretched out. I don't know that I slept. At some point
I found myself back in the middle of *The Peabody Sisters*. How I love
that book. Have I told you about it?

Sarah   Yes, many times.

Max   That Elizabeth—the oldest. She was a go-getter. And Sophie as
I recall, Sophie was always sick until Nathaniel Hawthorne came to the
house when all of a sudden she'd revive. Poor Elizabeth. They suggest
she would have married Hawthorne until Sophie interfered. Bad luck,
I suppose. Have I told you about it, Sarah?

Sarah   You have.

Max   I think it's just a marvelous book by the way.

Sarah   "All the World's Just a Little Clock Shop". Tick tock. Tick tock.

Max   Marvelous.

Sarah (*quietly*)   I'd be happy for you to tell me about it forever.

Max   What was that?

Sarah   Keep going.

Max   Well, as I recall the father became an unsuccessful doctor and the
mother had an awful lot of spunk to her.

Sarah   You see, there is a part of me that believes that if I just keep
writing this play my grandfather cannot die.

Or if I'm being completely honest—that I won't die.
That the various little ways my body has started to let me down—
the persistent pain in the ball of right my foot, the way
my teeth hurt when I run, that I can't read without
moving a light closer and then further from the page—that these little
failings don't mean anything.
As though I am Scheherazade, and the king holding the knife to my
throat is … time.
And yet here we are on page 194.
Or page 222 depending on font size, and margins.
You never really know how far along you are.

In the show that Evan saw, the elephant and the pig realize at some point
that they're in a play. And they become very existentially anxious about
this, about the play coming to an end. And about how to make the most
of the time they have left.

And the other day I was trying to explain to Evan how perception affects our experience of time. I said that the same day might feel much longer to him than it does to me. That for him time is big and unbreakable and expanding, like a universe.

He responded that he would very much like me to print out a picture for him of a cake.

Not long ago, Evan asked when he'd get to see heaven and what it looks like. John said that for him it would involve an endless variety of food trucks lining some beautiful beach. My husband loves nothing more than gourmet street food and weird fusions of exotic cuisines. Once a week he eats the best thing he's ever had in his life. So really John has made a heaven of earth.

I fear that sometimes I manage to make an earth of heaven.

Evan said that his heaven is a room full of cakes.

Evan   Cakes in the shape of doors. With knobs that help you get in.

Sarah   Get in where?

Evan   To heaven. Which is like The Liberty Science Center, only it's a circus tent that smells like chocolate.

Sarah   So heaven is like the *Great British Baking Show*.

Evan   Yes, Mom! Can we watch it again? The one with the icky sticky cake that broke.

Susan   Yes, I told him about heaven. What's wrong with that? … I also told him that some people think the world might not exist in the not too distant future. Climate change and all that. The polar ice caps.

Sarah   You didn't.

Susan   Don't worry; I don't think he entirely understood.

Sarah (*slightly annoyed*)   How did you explain heaven to him?

Susan   He seemed … unsettled by the idea that a person could just leave and never come back. And I didn't want him to think they were just nowhere all of a sudden.

Sarah   Is that what *you* believe?

Susan   Oh I don't know. Maybe. Your father does.

Jim   I do. I think we go nowhere. We end up nowhere.

Susan   I don't know. Maybe there's a reason so many people have believed in something like heaven for so long.

Jim   Fear.

Susan   Maybe. Or maybe not.

Jim   Of course it's fear. Which is why it's so remarkable that your grandfather is as cheerful as he is, at his age. We should all be so lucky.

Sarah   You don't think he's afraid?

Jim   No, he is. That's *why* it's so remarkable.

Sarah   The night before I leave for work on the west coast, Evan says:

Evan   Mom. Mom!! When you go away I miss you terribly.

Sarah   Just kill me now.

Evan   There can be a first day and there can be a last day when you're away. But no middle day.

Sarah   I'm afraid there have to be a couple middle days.

Evan   What are the days of the week again?

Sarah   This is his relationship to time. Still so new.

Evan   Monday
Sunday
Wednesday
Saturday
Friday

Sarah   John tells him he's missed a couple.

Evan   I'm going to miss you too much, Mom. Why are you always working?

Sarah   I'm going to miss you too much too.

Evan   How about when you're away, we connect the days with a string. Or with the Brooklyn Bridge.
And throw the bridge into the earth and that will connect the days.
And then you can come back.
That's an idea I just got. It's a good idea, Mom.

Will you do that?

Sarah   I will do that.

Evan   Okay. Then I'll let you go.

Sarah   Our perception of time changes our experience of time, changes *time* maybe. We have to believe this. That what we experience is, to some degree, what is. And so the experience of time speeding up is real.

Susan   You think time's going fast for *you*?

Sarah   Sometimes, unbidden, I imagine one of my parents has died and I find myself in tears in the middle of the night or in the middle of the street; it feels like the world is irrevocably broken, already, just *imagining* it.

Jim (*interrupting her*)   No, it's not retiring. I don't think of it that way. Just slowing down a bit. Consulting is not gonna be without its challenges.

Sarah   Of course not.

Jim   I anticipate a considerable number of hours each week. I wouldn't really call that retirement.

Susan *is on a different part of the stage. These are two separate conversations.*

Susan (*between us*)   Oh yeah. Yup. Your father is retiring.

Sarah   Well, that's not what he—

Jim   But it's going to be great fun to pick Evan up from school sometimes. I'll so enjoy doing things like that more often. Now that I'll have the time.

Susan   When I left the law I had no compunction about it. *I* never looked back.

Sarah   Because you didn't like it.

Susan   It's going to be harder for your father. And I'll tell you my worry is that he's just going to be *around* so much, you know? Hanging around.

Jim   You know, I'm very much looking forward to spending time with your mother during the days. We can go to the movies in the middle of a Tuesday.

Susan   It's just that I have my routines, you know?

Jim   I'm not retiring. Let's not call it that.

Sarah   No, you're just switching jobs. That's all.

(*To the audience, casual.*)

My father is just switching jobs and my grandfather is just … you know, turning 100. When I started writing this, he was getting weaker. But now, somehow, he's *100 years old*.

Max   Just like Sophie Peabody. I revived. Maybe soon *I'll* marry Nathaniel Hawthorne.

Sarah   It's April 28, 2018. My grandfather's birthday. We go down to Washington on the train, which delights Evan as trains have replaced cakes as his current obsession. He can't get enough of trains. Usually he is holding toy trains, one in each hand, and they transport his eighty-one imaginary friends. Today we are bringing all those teeny-tiny people with us on the Amtrak to DC. But it's not a pleasant ride. Evan, almost five now, wants things to be just so. He is not subtle about this:

Evan   I need things to be exactly as I want them. I need to control everything.

Sarah   He is unyielding. If he doesn't get a seat by a window. If he isn't held up on the platform to watch the train coming or going in just the right way. If he can't hold his trains or his brother tries to steal them. If he doesn't get one of the three foods he's willing to eat.

I mean, where does this come from in him?

Susan   Sarah, can I say something to you? I don't want you to take it the wrong way.

Sarah   That's never the start of something that's gonna go well.

Susan   No it's just, don't you think …

Sarah   What?

Susan   Just that on this visit … maybe don't do the play stuff. You know, taking notes while we talk and all that.

Sarah   The play *stuff*?

Susan   I know you're always getting inspiration from everywhere, and that's great; it really is … I just worry that your father and I could end up characters in some play. You know? Also, this is a special weekend, and …

Sarah   Well, are *you* gonna record grandpa then? I just think *someone* should be, like …

Susan   The thing is I don't think he wants to be recorded, or videotaped.

Sarah (*is she this out of touch?*)   Video-taped?

Susan   Streamed, whatever—it's just that he's so self-conscious about the way he looks now. But we'll do it sometime.

Sarah   Sometime is, like, now, isn't it?

Susan   I don't know. It might be.

Sarah   He's a *hundred*.

Susan (*quietly*)   I know. I'm just trying not to …

Sarah   Not to what?

Susan   Let it all in so much, maybe.

Beat.

Sarah   Will you ask him questions at least. He can't hear me at all. Will you think of some questions?

Susan *addresses* **Max**.

Susan   So Dad, how long did it take before you and Mom got engaged?

Sarah   This is before dinner, when a few of us are sitting together in my aunt's garden on this beautiful early spring evening. I am taking notes, but subtly.

Susan   … Dad?

Max   Long.

Susan   Before you were even engaged to be married? Is that because you were quite young?

Max   Young, undecided, you know, really, all those things.

Sarah   How old were you when you met Grandma?

Beat, then much louder.

I said, how old were you when—

Max   I heard you, Sarah, there's no need to shout. It was my freshman year in college.

Sarah   And she was younger … ?

Susan   Oh she was a fair bit younger.

Max   I believe we met at a freshman basketball game. And Ralph Goldwater—

Sarah   Oh yeah, Ralph Goldwater! He introduced you?

Susan   Ralph went to camp with Rose.

Sarah   So he introduced you and then you, like, chatted after the game?

Max   Yup, yup.

Sarah   And then you asked her out at some point?

Max (*laughing at himself*)   I don't know if I asked her out or if she asked herself out.

Sarah   Is that right?

Max   I was very un-aggressive.

Sarah   Were you shy?

Susan   He wasn't shy. He wasn't un-aggressive. This is a myth.

Max   I'm sure you've heard this story.

Sarah   What?

Max   Of my being thrown out of camp.

Sarah   Have I heard it?

Max   It was the night before—two nights before we were due to go home—and I had a date.

Susan   With Dippy Zelnick.

Sarah   Ohhh. I have heard this story. You snuck out, right? You snuck over to see Dippy.

Max   I got back to my bunk at 5 or 6 o'clock in the morning and soon I was awakened by the director of the camp and he said "Mr. Aarons you are being punished for tarnishing the reputation of the camp." He punished me and only me, when there were two others. In my shy way I guess I *was* the ringleader. Okay?

Sarah   So you weren't that shy.

Max   Well if you're a good athlete you're a ringleader. And they sent me home on the milk train.

Susan How old were you? Fifteen?

Max Something like that. But the best part of the story, the part I like best of all, when my father met the train, he laughed, and he said "I never thought I'd have a son who'd be such a great lover."

(*Sighing, wistful.*)

I had a ... I was very lucky. I had very nice parents.
... Hard to believe they've been gone fifty years now.

Susan Is it hard to believe you're a hundred, Dad?

Max Yes. And also no.

Sarah I remember when you turned seventy you said your birthdays were gonna start going backwards. Which would put you at forty now. Do you remember being forty?

Max Honestly, Sarah?

She nods.

No.

Sarah The other day my parents called. My father's voice was shaky. He said:

Jim It was awful. I woke up and the world was spinning. I could barely see. I couldn't walk to the bathroom. It was so intense that I actually threw up ...

Sarah What? What happened?

Jim (*hard to admit*) I was just ... I mean, I was terrified.

Sarah You were terrified?

Susan Which of course made me terrified.

Sarah Right.

Jim I was so scared I went straight to the ER. I mean, how could the world move like that. In my whole life I've never ...

Susan I didn't know what to do. Which isn't a feeling I'm accustomed to ...

Sarah (*quietly/fearfully*) So what did they say.

Jim They said it was some kind of benign vertigo.

Susan   So it's benign, which is obviously a good thing.

Jim   But apparently once it happens you're at a greater risk of it happening again.

Sarah   Okay.
… But it probably won't. Right?

Susan   Well, we certainly hope not. It was awful.

Jim   I think your mother started planning for life without me.

Susan   Of course I'd move in with you guys right away.

Sarah   With us?

Susan   I'm kidding, Sarah. I'd wait a few weeks at least.

Sarah   Hilarious, Mom.

Jim   No, really it was … bracing. This reminder that one morning you can wake up … and everything's different.

Susan   It's true. We just never imagined when we met—

Jim   At eighteen.

Susan   That one day we'd be this old. People in our generation think we'll never die. It's a Baby Boomer thing. We were the original young people. Or so it felt to us. And we were going to take over the world. And we did. But now … .

Sarah   In the backyard, my father is playing Evan a song on his phone. They'd been looking for songs about trains. When I get out there they've already listened to this one ten times. It's called "The City of New Orleans". Maybe you know it: (*She sings*) "Good morning America, how are ya? Say don't you know me; I'm your native son … "

Evan   Mom! I am in love with this song.

Sarah   Are you? Wow.

Evan   It was written by Steve Goodman in 1971. And do you know what? Steve Goodman is dead now. He died when he was thirty-six which is younger than you, Mom.

Sarah   I shoot my father a look. He shrugs.

Evan *lies down on the ground.*

Evan   Like this.

Sarah What are you doing?

Evan I'm Steve Goodman. I'm dead, Mom.

Sarah But something about this is too ...

No. Get up, I say. Get up right now.

Evan I can't get up. I'm dead. I'm Steve Goodman.

Sarah Get up, Evan!

Evan I'm never gonna get up again! That's what it means to be dead!! Don't you understand that, Mom?

Sarah (*to the audience, unsettled*) What?

Evan Mom.

Sarah What.

Evan (*more quietly, gently*) Don't you understand?

Sarah Stand up, honey. I need you to stand up now.

Evan There's a difference between knowing you're going to *die*, and *knowing* you're going to die.

Sarah What?

Evan Did you hear me?

Sarah Yes, I think, I, but ... I'm confused. Who are you all of a sudden?

Evan I'm growing up, Mom.

Sarah ... Oh right.

Evan And there's a difference between knowing you're going to *die*, and *knowing* you're going to die.

Sarah What is that? What's that from?

Evan It's not from anything. Not everything has to be from something else.

Sarah No I know that but ...

Evan Mom, why are you writing a play about me?

A breath.

Sarah (*to the audience*) Maybe all of this is an attempt to stave off the forward march of time.

Evan   I don't think you can do that. I mean, once the train has left the station …

Sarah   Wait—it *was* from something! *Three Tall Women*. "There's a difference between knowing you're going to *die*, and *knowing* you're going to die."

Evan   I don't know, Mom. I'm just a kid.

Sarah   Are you?

Evan   Also, my name isn't Evan. Your name isn't Sarah. Dad is most definitely not named John.

Sarah   I know.

Evan   Are we hiding or something?

Sarah (*confused*)   Maybe. I think so. I mean, yes.

Evan   From what?

Sarah (*to the audience*)   I watch as Evan plays hide and seek with his cousins in the backyard. He is hiding. They count: "5 4 3 2 1 ready or not here I come." And just like that, he pops out from behind a planter.

Evan   Here I am!! I'm over here.

Susan (*bemused/judgy*)   It's a very hard concept apparently, hide and seek. But it must snap in at some point.

Then, to **Evan**.

Evan, you have to stay where you are until someone finds you!

Evan   But I didn't want to be alone.

A cake is wheeled out onto the stage.

Evan   Cake!! Grandma, there's a cake! Do you see it?

Susan (*hushed, so Max doesn't hear*)   I do—I see it!

She puts her finger to her lips to quiet **Evan** *as they bring out the cake. The lights dim; lanterns appear across the stage. Stars, maybe.*
Evan, **Susan** *and* **Sarah** *sing "Happy Birthday" to* **Max**, *each of them referring to him by what he is to them—i.e. Dad/Grandpa/ Great-Grandpa.)*

Sarah   And then out of nowhere, it's night. Which can happen all of a sudden, in theater, and in life.

And we're sitting in the backyard, under lanterns, eating cake off paper plates.

Max   You know there's really no excuse, Sarah. And it is my birthday …

Sarah   A familiar glint in his eye. An expression I haven't seen since … well, I can't remember when.

Max   It's not like I'm getting any younger. If you've noticed. But I'll just keep waiting, I guess.

Sarah   Waiting for what?

Max   My starring role.

I think it would have to be a leading man, don't you? An uncommonly handsome *young* fellow with a mellifluous singing voice.

Beat.

Sarah (*quietly*)   Is that what you want? A starring role?

Evan   What's a starring role? I think I'd like a starring role. Is it sad that Steve Goodman died? I *hate* tunafish. Benjamin still doesn't say that many words. When will he stop being a baby? … What time will it be tomorrow?

Sarah   Sweetie, I'm trying to talk to Grandpa. Okay?

Evan   You mean Great-grandpa.

Sarah   Well yes, but he's my grandpa.

Evan   No, because one person can't be two things.

Sarah   Half our mother, half our father. One foot on earth and one in the grave.

Evan   Why can't I talk to you, Mom?? Why are you always talking to someone else??

He glares out at the audience, accusatorily.

Sarah   I always want to talk to you, Evan, it's just that …

Evan (*turning abruptly to* **Max**)   When are you going to die so I can talk to my Mom?

Max   What was that?

Evan   When are you going to die?

Max   … Do you want me to die, Evan?

Evan   No. But are you going to?

Max   Yes.

Evan   When?

Max   Soon.

Evan   Okay but I don't know when soon is. I don't understand "soon."

Max   You will, soon enough.

Evan   That confuses me. I'm confused.
… And I'm scared. Are you scared?

Beat.

Max   I *am* scared.

Evan   Like the way I am about being in a room by myself, or going to the potty, or falling asleep?

Max   Something like that.

Evan   And I'm a little bit scared about dying but also I really like cake and my heaven has cake in it.

Max (*singing, gently*)   *"Nothing's gonna harm you. Not while I'm around."*

Evan   I hope your heaven has cake too.

Max   Yes, when all is said and done there are compensations. And the kids, no doubt, are compensations for what goes on.

Evan   When is soon? Like … when we go back on the train to New York will we ever see you again?

Susan   Evan, maybe it's time for bed, honey.

Evan   But I have questions.

Susan (*affectionately*)   I'm not sure there's enough time in the world for all your questions.

Evan (*to Max, quietly*)   Will I ever see you again?

Beat.

Max (*singing, quietly*)
If ever I would leave you, it wouldn't be in summer.

Seeing you in summer, I never would go.
Oh what a beautiful mornin', oh what a beautiful day ...
The rain may never fall till after sundown.
By eight, the morning fog must disappear.
In short, there's simply not
A more congenial spot/

Sarah Grandpa?/

Max
For happily-ever-aftering than here /
In Camelot.

Susan Dad, what are you ... /

Max
Try to remember the kind of September
When life was slow and oh, so mellow.
Try to remember the kind of September

Max *and* **Sarah**
When grass was green and grain was yellow.
Try to remember the kind of September
When you were a tender and callow fellow.
Try to remember, and if you remember

Sarah Then follow.

Max Will you turn me into a song, Anna.

Sarah I'm trying.

A breath.

A song that never ends.

Beat.

Max ... No. It can end.

Sarah What?

Max I never knew a person could get this tired.

Sarah What are you—

Susan Do you want to take your hiatus now, Dad?

Max By the way that is such a lie: "The best is yet to be."

All sleeping. Sleeping on the hill.

Susan   Dad?

Max   "Our birth is but a sleep and a forgetting ... "

Sarah   Wordsworth.

Max   "Heaven lies about us in our infancy."

Sarah (*to the audience, with urgency*)   You give birth and your body opens—at once the most physical and the most disembodied moment you will ever know. It's very hard not to believe in something, God, maybe, after giving birth to a baby.

The whole time reminded that you have a body. A body you will be free of one day. That will free itself of you. Because this is what bodies do.

Max   "Shades of the prison house begin to close upon the growing boy."

Susan (*now with so much affection*)   This is what he's always been like. Everything done his way, on his terms.

Max (*as in, "I have to go"*)   Getting old sucks. What can I say.

Susan   But you've done it so well, Dad.

Max (*quietly, to the audience, not at all performative; he's leaving the world*)

> *When I am dead, my dearest,*
> *Sing no sad songs for me;*
> *Plant thou no roses at my head,*
> *Nor shady cypress tree:*
> *Be the green grass above me*
> *With showers and dewdrops wet;*
> *And if thou wilt, remember,*
> *And if thou wilt, forget.*

Susan   I think he's withdrawing.

Sarah   No. I don't think so.

Max

> *I shall not see the shadows,*
> *I shall not feel the rain;*
> *I shall not hear the nightingale*
> *Sing on, as if in pain ...*
> *And dreaming through the twilight*
> *that doth not rise nor set,*

Haply I may remember,
And haply may forget.

Sarah (*trying to stop him from leaving*)   No, don't go—

Susan (*quietly, as in "let him go"*)   Sarah.

Sarah (*abruptly, desperately*)   Okay, then how about, when you're
away, we connect the days with a string.
Or with the Brooklyn Bridge.
We could throw the bridge into the earth so it connects the days.
And then, whenever you want to, you can come back.
Will you do that? It's an idea I just had. I think it's a good idea.

Beat.

Max   … I will do that.

Beat.

Sarah (*the hardest thing she's ever done*)   Okay.

Then I'll let you go.

The lights shift, almost imperceptibly.

Sarah   In one version of the myth of the Minotaur, every day he passes
by the one place where he could escape the labyrinth only he doesn't
know it because it looks exactly like every other place. And there's
a poem by W. S. Merwin, a poem about how every year we pass the
anniversary of the day we will die.

Only we don't know it.

It could be today, as I write this, suspended in time, putting the Minotaur
back in a play, at the very end now. Can you see him, up on the stage?

An animal unlucky enough to understand his lot.

And an elephant and a pig, living out the rest of their days.

Susan   I do wish you could go easier on yourself, honey. There's so
much I wish you could just let go. The truth is, most things don't matter.
And even the things that do, you forget. So it's simply not worth the
anxiety. When you look back, it all looks kind of good, actually.

Sarah   Who are you? Who took my mother?
I want *my* mother.

Susan   Oh my Sarah.

She sings.

"To me you are so wonderful."

Sarah   The waiting rooms and the hotels and the lanterns and the bridges and a little clock shop tick tock tick tock.

Benjamin whose thighs seem to double in size each day.

His older brother whose fears are becoming more and more real.

The terror that I remember moving through me every day as a child.

The bullet train that brings us to this mysterious place and then takes us away again.

Evan   Mom.

Sarah   You see things that day, the day you give birth, the days just after.

Evan   I'm going to say opposites ... okay?

Sarah   For a little while maybe you are outside of time.

Evan   I'm saying opposites. Young and old. Tall and short ... Real and pretend.

Sarah (*looking at* **Evan**)   One morning, there's your son, sitting on the edge of your bed, *an old man.* And it breaks your heart. There's a reason why we don't see our children get old.

Evan (*he's growing up*)   Awake and asleep. Open and shut. Simple and complicated. Translucent and ... opaque.

Sarah   But we do watch them grow. And in this way, they make time visible.

Evan (*quietly, simply, with no urgency*)   Mom. Look at me.

Sarah (*a discovery*)   This is the way we *make* time.

Evan   Happy and sad. Quiet and loud. Birth and ...

Sarah   Evan.

Evan   Monday Tuesday Wednesday Thursday Friday Saturday Sunday

Sarah (*with deep pleasure, but bittersweet*)   You did it.

Evan   It's now, Mom. You have to pay attention to me. This is the only now there is.

Sarah   ... Okay, honey.
I'm here.
With you.
And look at us.
We're up on the stage.
Together.

Together, they look out at the theater, at the audience, at the world, in wonder, taking it all in.

Evan   Do we sing a little song?

Sarah   We do.

Sarah *takes* **Evan**'s *hand. They look at each other with so much love. We hear a recording of a woman and a child singing a verse of "The City of New Orleans."*

> *Good morning, America*
> *How are you?*
> *Say don't you know me? I'm your native son*
> *I'm the train they call the city of New Orleans*
> *And I'll be gone five hundred miles when the day is done.*

By the time we've reached the end of the song the lights have dimmed to black.

End of play